EcoNest

Eco

CREATING SUSTAINABLE SANCTUARIES
OF CLAY, STRAW, AND TIMBER

Nest

Paula Baker-Laporte and Robert Laporte

Foreword by Robyn Griggs Lawrence

Gibbs Smith, Publisher
Salt Lake City

First Edition

09 08 07 06 05   5 4 3 2 1

Published by
Gibbs Smith, Publisher
P.O. Box 667
Layton, Utah 84041

Orders: 1.800.748.5439
www.gibbs-smith.com

Designed by Steven Rachwal
Printed and bound in China

Quote on page 47 from *The Nest,* © 1999 by Maryjo Koch. Text quoted
from introduction by Gretel Ehrlich. Published by Stewart, Tabori, and
Chang. Used with permission. All rights reserved.

Library of Congress Cataloging-in-Publication Data

Baker-Laporte, Paula, 1953-
  Econest : creating sustainable sanctuaries of clay, straw, and timber /
Paula Baker-Laporte and Robert Laporte.— 1st ed.
      p. cm.
  Includes bibliographical references and index.
  ISBN 1-58685-691-X
 1. Ecological houses. 2. Earth houses. 3. Straw bale houses. 4.
Sustainable buildings. 5. Appropriate technology. 6. Wooden-frame
houses.
I. Laporte, Robert (Robert M.), 1955- II. Title.
  TH4860.B35 2005
  690'.8—dc22
                                    2005010336

CONTENTS

6
Foreword

8
Acknowledgments

9
Introduction: What is an Econest?

10
Building with Light Clay/Straw

14
The Econest System for Clay/Straw Building

24
Building for Health Naturally

30
The Elements of Econest Design and Construction

36
Workshops

39
Making It Happen For You

40
Eight Common Questions About Econests

42
Case Studies

126
Resources

136
Index

FOREWORD

Seven years ago I'd just taken on this overwhelming position as editor in chief of *Natural Home* magazine (now *Natural Home & Garden*). A newbie to this whole green building thing, I was slowly seeking out the movers and shakers, the pioneers who'd been with it from the beginning. Everyone was amazingly generous, taking the time to educate me and introduce me to others. I soon learned that that's what this movement is all about: innovating, learning, and passing it all on—without hesitancy. This isn't a world of trade secrets, but one of alliances. That's a key part of what makes green building so much fun.

In the course of my discoveries, I kept running into the names *Robert Laporte* and *Paula Baker-Laporte,* two prime examples of the power of these alliances (although they took it a little bit further than most with their additional romantic partnership). This incredible team, I learned, had been at the core of the movement for many years, developing and improving clay/straw building techniques and generally forwarding the action in creating healthy, sustainable homes for everyone. Paula, a Bau-biologist, and Robert, a timber framer, have been perfecting the art of healthy, enlightened, environmentally sound building techniques for many, many years.

Over the past seven years, we've featured many of Robert and Paula's econest homes in the pages of *Natural Home & Garden.* I'm fondest, I think, of one of Robert's first houses, featured on page 44, which he built nearly two decades ago while he was living in Fairfield, Iowa. This is the house that launched Robert's career as a green builder and teacher, and the epiphany that led him to build it is a familiar one for many of us. (The circumstances may differ, but we've all had "the moment" when we realized the crucial importance of creating homes that nurture mind, body, and soul.) Robert came to his moment during a lecture in which Maharishi Mahesh Yogi was explaining *vastu,* the ancient Indian art of creating prosperity, health, and tranquility through the orientation, proportion, and placement of buildings. "We build in such a way that everything nourishes everything," the spiritual guru said.

Robert set out to build a home using local, natural, unprocessed materials, participating in every aspect of the building process rather than passing off the messy, toxic jobs such as Sheetrocking and painting. The result is a fortress against Iowa's wicked winters and sultry summers (even without air-conditioning), a place whose soul is bared in thick, nurturing walls and silky wood beams. I visited that house one late-July day, and I truly didn't want to leave.

The same thing happened a couple years later, when I visited Paula and Robert's fabulous clay/straw home in Tesuque, New Mexico (page 68). The home is superbly designed to take advantage of its site and the climate. Spacious and uncluttered, full of stunning aesthetic finishes such as natural earthen plasters, it's also mechanically ingenious, taking full advantage of the sun and foot-thick straw-clay walls. "This house will last for 500 years," Robert said to me in one of my favorite quotes of all time. "And if it's an energy hog for 500 years, it will be condemned in hell. So if you build well—so that a house lasts longer—you have a bigger responsibility."

More than anything, though, Paula and Robert's house is a tribute to their mutual respect, and Robert's beautiful acknowledgment of Paula's talent in designing it actually brought tears to my eyes. The fact is, I never leave an interaction with Paula and Robert without being completely touched and inspired, both professionally and personally. They've not only given me the gift of their professional wisdom, but they've inadvertently taught me about partnership and love, the life that comes into *anything* when two people are working with passion and open hearts. That's a gift to the world that will last for as long as their houses—and guarantee them a spot in heaven.

—ROBYN GRIGGS LAWRENCE, EDITOR IN CHIEF, *Natural Home & Garden*

ACKNOWLEDGMENTS

We would like to acknowledge those giants and pioneers of building and architecture too numerous to mention, upon whose shoulders we humbly stand. Many thanks to our European teachers and inspirations: Franz Volhard, Uli Rohlen, and Peter Breidenbach, founder of Claytech Corporation, for their pioneering work with straw and clay; Dr. Anton Schneider, founder of Bau-biologie, and our dear friend Helmut Ziehe, who brought Bau-biologie to North America and founded the Institute of Bau-biologie and Ecology. Thanks to David Pearson who has moved and inspired us with his many books on natural building.

On the North American front we would like to acknowledge Catherine Wanek and Ianto Evans for bringing natural builders together at the early colloquiums. Special thanks to Robyn Griggs Lawrence for putting natural building in the hearts and minds of America through *Natural Home and Garden* magazine and for her personal contribution in writing the foreword of this book.

Robert would like to give special acknowledgment to Tedd Benson, father of the North American timberframe revival, and company, who took a young apprentice under their generous wings and taught him the art and craft of timber frame.

Thank you to the family at Gibbs Smith, Publisher, with special thanks to Christopher Robbins for finding us and proposing this book, to Johanna Buchert Smith, our editor, and to Gibbs Smith, for fostering a creative atmosphere for all manner of inquiry.

Thank you to all those who have participated in the building experience with us over the years and special thanks to those who have shared that experience in the pages of this book. Thank you to Steve Vessey for bringing his phenomenal craftsmanship, good humor, and companionship to so many econest projects. Robert is especially grateful for Steve's endurance and patience during those early groundbreaking and backbreaking stages of "product development." Thanks too to Steve Lawrence, we both enjoy working with you so much!

Thank you, David Madden for your wonderful illustrations; Laurie Dickson for your photos of our work over the years; and thank you to Margaret for always being there behind the scenes, the only one who knows where to find everything!

Finally, thank you to Phil Fisher, designer, and William Laporte, builder. It's in our genes!

INTRODUCTION

WHAT IS AN ECONEST?

The original ecological nest builders:
a swallow with her babies in a mud/fiber nest.

A bird builds its nest using the materials at hand to create a perfect shelter for its bioregion. It doesn't fly to the next state for twigs nor does it build a home that is bigger than it needs. Instinctively it creates an environment that is nurturing, nontoxic, and free of synthetic chemicals, bearing no mortgage, creating no waste and neither borrowing nor stealing resources from future generations. These exemplary owner/builders know how to build and repair their own shelters. When they have no more use for their nests, the building materials decompose, becoming fertile ground for nature's regenerative miracle.

Humans, too, have a nesting instinct. Creating a "nest" connotes making a shelter that is cozy and nurturing … a place of one's own in the world. *Econest* is the name we have given to homes that we design and build for our clients and ourselves. Like the bird nests that inspired it, the econest embodies our efforts to build respectfully, in appreciation of the harmony and beauty of nature, and in a way that uses nature's resources so as to consume less energy, create less waste, nurture our health, enrich our senses, and improve the quality of our lives. We have turned to preindustrial building materials and techniques, reevaluated them in terms of modern necessities and comforts and found them to be not only viable, but in many ways superior to the mass-manufactured products that make up the palette of standard building materials today.

As an architect-and-builder team, our life's work has been to nurture the nesting instinct in our clients while shepherding them through the complex process of creating a home. This odyssey often represents the largest investment that they will ever make — financially, creatively, and emotionally. We dedicate this book to those who have, together with us, pioneered in creating econest homes.

BUILDING WITH LIGHT CLAY/STRAW

HISTORICAL OVERVIEW

Light clay/straw (or "light loam" construction, a more accurate translation of the German *leichtlehmbau*) evolved in Germany from heavier clay construction known as *wattle and daub*. Wattle and daub was commonly used throughout Europe and Asia as infill between timbers, and examples date back to the earliest known buildings. The use of wattle and daub remains a common building practice today among indigenous cultures in Europe, Asia, and Africa. Post–World War II reconstruction in Germany brought with it the innovation of "lightening" the clay infill by adding much more straw, thus increasing the insulation value of the walls. In these early examples light clay/straw was primarily used as an infill system between structural members.

Robert first studied this technique in 1990 when he went to Germany in search of a natural wall system for his timberframe structures. Since that time he has invented and continually refined a system for completely wrapping his own timberframe structures with the light clay/straw mixture. This process, which has been termed "outsulation," has produced a thermally efficient monolithic envelope. The envelope is virtually free of the thermal bridging that occurs in most standard North American home construction where insulation is stuffed between studs.

An 800-year-old timberframe and wattle-and-daub structure that has been continuously occupied in Limburg an der Lahn, Germany.

At the time of this writing there are several builders working with *leichtlehmbau* in North America using a variety of fibers (straw, wood chip, and hemp, to name a few). In the text that follows, we will concentrate on the econest clay/straw technique.

RECENT TEST RESULTS

How does light clay/straw stack up when compared to modern, manufactured building materials? Our experience of building and living in econests tells us that it is exceptionally comfortable: warm in the winter, cool in the summer, and stable in temperature, changing only very slowly as weather conditions outside cycle through daily and seasonal extremes.

Until very recently, however, the only scientific information about the performance of light clay/straw as an insulating wall system was based on testing carried out in Germany (see Franz Volhard's book *Leichtlehmbau alter Baustoff-neue Technik*, Karlsruhe, Germany: Verlag C. F. Muller, 1998, p. 116). But in North America officials tend to recognize only test results done in specific laboratories in the United States and Canada. Because standardized testing for building materials in North America is extremely expensive, building-product manufacturers, who stand to make large profits selling their products, are usually the test sponsors. Clay/straw and other nonproprietary building systems composed of naturally found materials are the underfinanced orphans of an industrialized building culture.

At the time of this writing, the first scientific testing of light clay/straw in both Canada and the United States is in progress. Early results can now substantiate our subjective experience with objective scientific data. This scientific backing is important when working with building officials who

The Kinkaku-Ji Temple, a fifteenth-century Japanese timberframe structure with earthen-infill walls.

may consider these ancient natural materials to be "experimental" or "alternative."

A brief summary of the recent studies follows.

THERMAL RESISTANCE OF LIGHT CLAY/STRAW

Thermal resistance, or R-value, is the measure of the ability of a material at a specified thickness to resist the transfer of heat. The higher the R-value, the greater the ability of a building material to insulate. Testing different materials under the same fixed atmospheric conditions allows us to make a comparison of these materials. Although R-value is only one of many factors determining energy efficiency and comfort performance of an indoor environment, it is the primary one that building officials in the United States consider when deciding if a building meets energy-efficiency requirements well enough to qualify for a building permit.

Recently the Canadian Mortgage and Housing Corporation (CMHC) provided a government grant to Joshua Thornton to research the physical characteristics of

Taken with infrared photography, these thermal images are of the front and back side of an adobe wall that surrounds a masonry oven in an econest. They show the amount of infrared radiation, or heat, being emitted from surfaces. The middle image was taken while a fire was burning in the oven. The image on the right was taken twelve hours after the fire was out. Note that the wall continues to store and radiate heat long after the fire has subsided. In effect, the entire wall becomes a radiant heater with a comfortable and very even distribution. These thermal images help us to see the invisible and illustrate why very little fuel is required to achieve a high level of thermal comfort in a home built with massive walls.

light clay/straw, or simply "clay/straw," as we will refer to the material henceforth. He has carried out his testing under the mentorship of Dr. John Straube, a respected building scientist at the University of Waterloo. They tested three densities of clay/straw and found that the average R-value for a 12-inch-thick wall with a density of 40 to 45 pounds per square foot is R-19. Test results also include data on vapor permeability, moisture storage, and fire resistance. (The CMHC study authored by Joshua Thornton may be viewed on our Web site, www.econest.com.) Concurrent testing with lighter mixtures of clay/straw by architect Lou Host-Jablonski of Madison, Wisconsin, in conjunction with the U.S. Forest Products Laboratory, also recorded acceptable thermal performance data. Both of these studies substantiate tests performed earlier in Europe.

These results are significant in two respects: First, they provide hard data to prove to building officials that at a certain density, the R-value of a 12-inch-thick clay/straw wall equals 6 inches of fiberglass batt insulation. In most areas of the country this is a sufficient R-value for an insulating wall to pass energy code and help pave the way for a building permit. Second, these results alone do not explain the true energy performance of clay/straw. We know from our experience that the energy performance of a 12-inch clay/straw wall is far greater than that of a standard 2 x 6 wall with 6 inches of fiberglass batt insulation. There are several reasons for this:

◉ In standard construction, fiberglass batt insulation is placed between wooden studs that are spaced at 16 or 24 inches on center. Each stud is a "thermal bridge" through which outside temperatures find their way more quickly to the inside of the building. So if we look at the overall energy performance of the wall, we find it would be less than the R-19 that the fiberglass batts contribute. A clay/straw wall in an econest is designed to wrap around the structure without interruption. As mentioned previously, we call this outsulation. There is very little thermal bridging, so the whole wall performs at the R-19 value.

◉ Another very important factor to the overall comfort level experienced in a clay/straw building is the role of thermal mass. When walls containing thousands of pounds of clay are heated by the sun, they will very slowly transfer the heat from the outside in, and by nighttime they will have a warming, moderating effect on the interior. Likewise, at night these walls will slowly cool, transferring the "coolness" to the interior during the heat of the day. This delayed reaction that works to our comfort advantage is called the flywheel effect. Its benefits are mostly experienced in climates such as the desert Southwest where there are large daytime-to-nighttime temperature differentials.

◉ In colder climates, where there is a long heating season, the thermal mass is also advantageous. When the space is heated the walls absorb and store the heat, creating a source of additional radiant heat and providing "surround comfort."

◉ In hot, dry climates a mass of earth has long been used as a storage mechanism to cool a space, as well. When the air in an interior environment is cooler than the exterior air, it will remain cooler longer if the surrounding walls store the temperature. For example, one would need to run an air conditioner constantly inside a tent on a hot day to remain cool. In an adobe building of the same size, however, it would be necessary to provide cool air only for short periods of time to maintain comfortable temperatures because the walls "store" the coolness instead of allowing it to escape. Whether the temperature differential is generated by ancient evaporative cooling towers of the Middle East or modern-day mechanical air-conditioning, massive walls will store the cold temperatures and provide comfort.

The Econest System for Clay/Straw Building

THE MATERIALS

There are different methods of constructing clay/straw walls. In any system there will be three components: a structural matrix, temporary or permanent formwork, and the clay/straw infill. When the technique was first introduced into North America in 1990, clay slip was poured onto a loose mixture of straw, hand-mixed with a pitchfork, and transported to the walls in wheelbarrows. Formwork was

heavy, awkward, and slow. Also, the original structural wall system was difficult to load and prone to excessive settling. Over the years Robert has developed a comprehensive and more automated system for building the walls, which has resulted in far more efficiency. We will briefly describe these techniques in the pages that follow.

Pouring clay slip onto straw.

Hand mixing a clay/straw slip mixture with pitchforks.

STRAW

Straw provides bulk, insulation, and tensile strength in a clay/straw wall system. Straw fiber has significant tensile strength, and its hollow structure traps air, thus providing effective insulation naturally. Several different types of straw are available. The best straw for building clay/straw walls is barley, followed by wheat. Because of their high water repellency and bulkiness, they compress less, so it takes less straw to build up the walls, there is less shrinkage, and the walls have a higher insulating value.

It is important to use materials that are locally available and, whenever possible, straw that is free of pesticides. Clay/straw walls have also been built successfully using rice and oat straw, but these walls take longer to build and require more straw. A 1,400-square-foot econest will require approximately 125 thirty-five-pound barley bales. By comparison, the same building using rice or oat straw would require approximately 25 percent more bales.

CLAY

We consider clay to be the Cadillac (and the Prius) of technologically advanced building materials. Clay is the glue that cements the straw fibers together into a monolithic wall. Clay encases each fiber of straw, protecting it from decay by drawing moisture away and releasing it into the air. The clay also provides the majority of the weight or mass to the wall.

Soils with sufficient clay content for wall building are abundantly available throughout most of North America. If there are birds in your neighborhood, such as swallows or robins, that build with fiber and mud, then the proper clay soils exist in your locality. For mixing clay/straw, the clay soil needs to be in a dry powdered or pulverized form and not in big, wet, heavy clods (as commonly found in wetter regions). Most landscape companies have a soil shredder that can granulate chunky clay into an acceptable pea size for use in wall building.

The optimal percentage of clay content in the soil used for building walls is 80 to 100 percent. Minimal clay content is 50 percent. How do you know how much clay is in your clay soil? There are some simple tests that you can perform yourself to gauge the content.

The ribbon test is a field test performed by taking a tablespoon of the dry soil and wetting it just enough so that it becomes malleable. If you can roll the sample into a pencil-sized cylinder without it falling apart, then the sample has at least a 50 percent clay content. If the ribbon can be bent to 90 degrees without breaking, the sample probably has more than 75 percent clay content. Finally, if the sample can mold into a ring without breaking, you have export-quality material! The greater the clay content, the stickier the clay/straw mix and the less soil required to build the walls. More elaborate testing is detailed in the books by Minke and Volhard listed on page 129.

The average 1,400-square-foot econest requires approximately 15 cubic yards of 75-percent-clay-content soil.

A student assembles a corner Larsen truss in a special miter jig.

CREATING THE MATRIX

The matrix is a light framework that wraps around the timber structure, facilitating form attachment and framing the openings. The matrix can also be designed to be a load-bearing structure where a timber frame is not used.

To achieve the desired wall thickness of 12 inches and to reduce wood consumption, Larsen trusses are utilized in the matrix. A Larsen, or ladder, truss consists of a pair of studs attached with plywood gussets. This configuration is most efficiently prefabricated in a jig. Larsen trusses can be spaced 48 inches on center when used in conjunction with a timber frame, or 24 inches on center when loadbearing.

Larsen trusses are the framework for thick monolithic walls.

A student fabricates a simple Larsen truss in a jig.

RIGHT » A clay/straw–timberframe wall section. 1. Metal roofing on waterproofing membrane. 2. Exterior plywood sheathing. 3. Cedar fascia on subfascia. 4. Rough-sawn wood soffit. 5. Earth plaster. 6. Stone veneer with sloped cap. 7. Insulated concrete forms, fully grouted with vertical reinforcing. 8. Concrete footing with horizontal reinforcing. 9. Perimeter footing drain set in gravel and covered with filter fabric. 10. Tongue-and-groove aspen ceiling. 11. Timber plate. 12. Stud with holes for stabilizing bar. 13. Timber post. 14. 12-inch clay/straw infill. 15. Sill plate. 16. Continuous reinforcing bar. 17. Plaster base coat. 18. Dowel. 19. Concrete pier under timbers, doweled into the foundation.

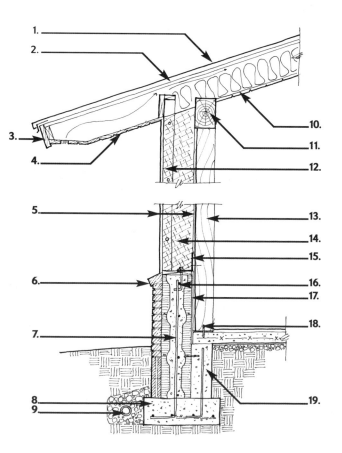

In a Larsen truss wall the space between the studs allows for an uninterrupted, or monolithic, wall. Thermal bridging and air infiltration are greatly reduced, as compared with conventional stud-framed construction.

Although clay/straw walls are used in a non-loadbearing capacity, once dry, the walls have considerable strength. It is conceivable that, with future structural testing, these walls will be classified as loadbearing by meeting or surpassing building codes for compressive and shear strength.

Once the Larsen trusses are erected and the matrix is completed, the walls are ready to receive formwork.

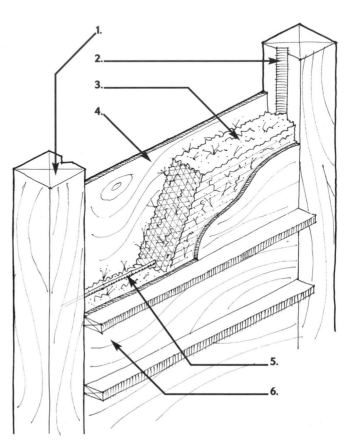

ABOVE » Clay/straw infill between timber frames can be used where a high standard of thermal performance is not required. 1. Exposed timber frame. 2. V-groove keyway. 3. Clay/straw infill. 4. Inside-formwork plywood. 5. Bamboo horizontal stabilizing bar. 6. Exterior-formwork plywood, with horizontal walers.

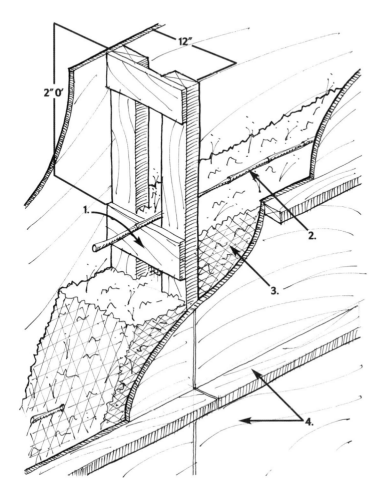

LEFT » Solid plywood forms on the inside and removable forms on the outside are secured to the Larsen truss. A horizontal bamboo bar is placed on the truss gusset. Each two-foot form is topped off with the clay/straw mixture. 1. A Larsen truss with two 2 x 3s and exterior plywood gussets at 2′0′. 2. A 3/4-inch diameter bamboo for horizontal reinforcing. 3. Clay/straw mixture. 4. Formwork of 3/4-inch plywood with 2 x 4 horizontal walers.

ABOVE » This econest's interior is fully formed, and the first exterior plywood form is in place on the matrix.

ABOVE » The first form is topped off and stabilized with bamboo.

ABOVE » The second form is keyed into the top of the first and screwed to the matrix.

ABOVE » Form 1 has been leapfrogged to become form 3.

ABOVE » A freshly completed wall capped off with a top plate; roof framing has already begun.

CREATING THE FORMWORK
"LEAPFROGGING UP THE WALL"

With the matrix completed, the interior wall is entirely covered with 3/4-inch plywood, which is screwed to the framing members of the matrix, forming a solid wall and leaving only large door and window openings exposed. Because this plywood is later reused for roof sheathing, it is kept in as large a size as is practical.

On the exterior, pairs of 24-inch-tall forms in various lengths are leapfrogged up the wall. The first form is screwed to the matrix, loaded, tamped, and stabilized with horizontal bamboo. The second form is installed above the first, loaded, tamped, and stabilized; then the first form is removed and installed above the second form. This leapfrogging process is repeated until the wall is completed. When any form is removed it is screeded down to smooth the wet clay/straw surface before pulling it away. Otherwise, straw fiber stuck to the form could be pulled out, leaving a shaggy wall surface. It is important that the formwork be removed as soon as possible, ideally the same day the wall is started, to allow for air circulation and rapid drying of the wall. If a building site is not naturally windy we often accelerate the initial drying phase by inducing air movement with high-velocity fans. Formwork left in place for more than two days will foster unnecessary mold growth under the plywood.

MAKING THE CLAY/STRAW MIXTURE
"PHARAOH'S FRIEND AND THE BLIND PILOT"

Making the clay/straw is a process of combining straw, water, and granulated clay into a homogeneous mixture ready for placing into the formwork. Density can be controlled by varying the clay content of the mixture and by increasing or decreasing the degree of tamping. Ideally, walls requiring more insulation, such as a north wall, will be of a lighter mix (30 to 40 pounds per cubic foot, or pcf). Conversely, south walls or interior walls, where more mass for heat storage is desirable, require a heavier mix (up to 60 pcf).

One of the keys to successful wall building is having enough mixed material on hand at all times to fully utilize the wall-stuffing labor force. At a workshop, "many hands make light work" indeed, and a very labor-intensive undertaking can occur with great speed if the clay/straw-mixture supply can keep up with the labor force demands. Allowing the mixed material to sit overnight or for several hours will make it stickier as the clay particles fully absorb the water. The stickier material will stay compressed with a minimal amount of compaction, whereas freshly mixed material will be "springier" and will require more labor to keep it compacted. The clay/straw tumbler, or "Pharaoh's friend," as inventors Alfred von Bachmayr and Joe MaGrath dubbed it, is a fairly simple but ingenious piece of equipment. It is created out of a corrugated metal cylinder 3 feet in diameter by 10 feet long, mounted on a motorized set of wheels. The whole assembly is then set at a slight incline so material tumbles forward and downward. Three rows of tines inside the cylinder mix the clay/straw and water as the material works its way from the feed end to an awaiting hopper at the discharge end. We highly recommend that anyone planning to build a clay/straw residence borrow, rent, or build one of these machines. (Refer to the Resources section on page 132 for Alfred von Bachmayr's contact information.) The alternative is to hand-mix the clay/straw with pitchforks, which will require almost twice as much labor and is most appropriate for small projects.

The first task in mixing the clay/straw is to build a proper staging area. Ideally, the crew at the mixing station will work like a well-rehearsed orchestra, with each member delivering his or her piece on cue. The key players in the clay/straw-mixing symphony are pilot, copilot, clay supplier, and straw supplier. We refer to the pilot as the "blind pilot," because if all the team members are doing their jobs he/she shouldn't need to look around for materials, and all materials will be within arm's reach. The pilot throws an armload of straw, a bucket of water, and several buckets of clay into the tumbler in rapid succession. Type of straw, type of clay soil, and desired density will vary on each site. Because of the variability of the materials it is the copilot's job to monitor the product coming out the end of the tumbler and give feedback to the pilot, such as "too wet," "more clay," "just right," and so on. The clay supplier's job is to shovel the right amount of clay from the clay pile into buckets and place them on the platform where the pilot can readily grab them. The pilot throws the clay down the throat of the tumbler and then tosses the bucket back to the digging area. The straw supplier's job is to break apart the bales of straw and place the supply so that the pilot can readily access an armload with minimal movement.

An electric clay/straw tumbler creates quiet and efficient production.

An organized and ergonomically planned mixing station is essential for efficient clay/straw production. 1. Baling platform: The baler loads straw bales from platform into hopper. Bale strings are removed and positioned for easy access. 2. Water tub: Hose supplies tub with water. 3. Digging area: Diggers fill buckets with dry clay and position it on platform. 4. Pilot's platform: The pilot adds the proper amounts of straw, water, and clay into the mixer. All materials are easily accessed. 5. Copilot's area: The slightly sloped mixer combines the ingredients and sends them into the hopper. The copilot is responsible for the quality control of the mix.

We have found that a rectangular, 200-gallon trough placed to one side of the pilot works well for providing the water in the clay/straw mix. The pilot is responsible for maintaining the supply and for adding a small amount of boric acid to the mix, as required. Boric acid is available in bulk and is added to retard mold growth while the clay/straw mixture is drying. Boric acid can be readily found in most grocery stores in the form of "20 Mule Team" laundry booster. We use one box per 200 gallons of water. This amount can be increased if drying conditions are less than optimal.

DELIVERING THE MATERIAL
"FORKLIFTS AND HOPPERS"

Another key to productive work is the efficient delivery of heavy material from the mixing station to the wall site. A forklift is used to transfer "hoppers" filled with the clay/straw mixture to scaffolding that has been set up adjacent to the perimeter wall.

A specially designed lightweight plywood hopper will hold approximately 500 pounds of material. Two keyways in

A forklift delivers clay/straw directly to where a wall is being loaded.

the back bottom of the hopper are designed for safely lifting and moving the heavy hoppers with a forklift.

When site conditions prohibit forklift access to the wall being built, wheelbarrows are used to shuttle the material along the scaffolding that encircles the building perimeter. On extremely challenging sites we recommend a crane for material delivery.

PLACING THE CLAY/STRAW IN THE FORMS
"LEARNING FROM SIR ISAAC NEWTON"

The laws of gravity can be friend or foe. It is far easier to drop tons of wet material into formwork than to lift it up into the formwork. Several years ago a very challenging site led to our rediscovery of this simple law of physics and it revolutionized the econest building technique. One way of using gravity to your advantage is to set up scaffolding so that the forklift can place the hoppers full of clay/straw as high as or higher than the wall being filled. It may take several hours to set up this favorable condition but once it is set, this is the quickest and least labor-intensive way to load a form because it minimizes heavy lifting. Dropping the clay/straw from a height also helps to compact it so that less stomping is required. Loading the forms is the most labor-intensive portion of the work, so a well-thought-out setup is invaluable.

From the hopper the clay/straw is placed into the wall cavity in a loose 6-inch layer. Standing inside the formwork with feet parallel to the wall, an individual can compact the loose material by walking and stomping on it, forward and backward two to three times, until the material no longer springs up. Tight areas next to studs are compacted with tampers fashioned out of two-by-fours. This process is repeated until the 24-inch-high form is filled. At this point

A worker loads a wheelbarrow for delivering clay/straw to areas inaccessible by forklift.

3/4-inch-diameter horizontal bamboo stabilizing bars are installed on top of the gussets or in holes drilled in the studs. The bamboo, secured in place, significantly reduces settlement and also adds lateral stability until the wall dries.

DRYING THE WALLS

Once the clay/straw walls are in place, they are left to dry thoroughly before receiving earthen plasters inside and out. It is not unusual to see some superficial mold on the surface of the drying wall. In fact, in the damper climate of Germany, Robert observed mushrooms sprouting from walls as a regular and accepted occurrence! Since every fiber of straw in a wheat field has mold spores on it, it is natural that these spores will begin to grow in wet conditions. However, once the dried walls are plastered, scientific testing has shown that the indoor air is free of any ambient mold from wall construction.

Bamboo is installed at the top of each lift.

Compressing the wall's clay/straw by stomping on it.

Of concern is that the drying process is sufficiently rapid to prevent decomposition of the straw fibers. This would only occur where atmospheric conditions remain extremely wet and dark. Clay/straw construction for 12-inch-thick walls is most viable in climates that have a significant dependable dry season of at least twelve weeks. Intermittent rainstorms during the drying period are not a significant setback due to the incredible wicking and drying power of clay.

Remarkably, a clay/straw wall comes equipped with its own natural built-in moisture meters. Soon after the wall has been placed, the seeds left in the straw begin to sprout. For a while the building resembles a vertical lawn. As the walls dry, these sprouts dry out and die. An agricultural instrument known as a bale probe will confirm when the walls have 19 percent or less moisture content and are ready to receive natural plasters. In the dry New Mexico climate, walls are always ready to plaster as soon as the normal construction sequencing permits, i.e., after at least twelve weeks of drying. In moister climates it may be prudent to plaster only the inside during the first season. The building can be inhabited while the exterior walls season over the first indoor heating cycle. In the finished home these "breathable" walls provide a constant slow exchange of water vapor, contributing to a stable and comfortable indoor environment.

The sprouts, which appear within a week of placing the wall, serve as a built-in moisture meter, dying off when the wall is too dry to support them. This is green building!

Wall drying can be accelerated with fans.

BUILDING FOR HEALTH NATURALLY

"Sick building syndrome," "multiple chemical sensitivities," "twentieth- (or twenty-first-) century disease," and "building-related illness" are all relatively new terms describing a relatively new and rapidly growing phenomenon: people becoming chronically ill due to chemical and biological toxins found inside modern homes and workplaces. Our homes should be our sanctuaries. They should nurture our well-being. They often do not. They certainly can!

CREATING THE MASS WALL ADVANTAGE

The post–WWII years ushered in the era of "better living through chemistry" and a booming building industry promised to be a proving ground for new and improved industrialized building products. These new products and systems rapidly replaced time-tested building techniques that had evolved and been perfected slowly over the centuries.

Unfortunately, new has not necessarily proven to be better. Scrutiny of our current human and ecological health has resulted in a reevaluation and revival of earth-based building methods such as rammed earth, cob, adobe, and clay/straw, which predate the changes in building technology and lifestyles that have led to sick building syndrome. Can these time-tested materials offer solutions to our newfound problems? The answer to this question is a resounding yes! Until very recent history all dwellings were made out of natural, locally available materials. These walls were "breathable," or "flow through," wall systems with hygric capacity so they could accept large amounts of water vapor safely without creating the moisture and mold problems associated with modern cavity wall construction.

The job of the exterior wall is to slow down temperature and moisture transfer so that the interior environment can be favorably modified for human comfort. Solid-mass walls, especially walls containing clay, have the ability to handle large amounts of vapor diffusion without any deterioration of the building fabric or performance because of the outstanding ability of clay to absorb, store, and then release moisture. Needless to say, a hollow stud wall of metal or wood does a very poor job of moderation without the addition of insulation. Industry-standard insulations such as fiberglass batts perform very poorly when moisture is allowed to travel through them. In addition, if enough water vapor passes into and condenses in the hollow cavity it will cause mold, decay, and eventual structural deterioration. To avoid this, insulated stud walls are most often constructed with moisture barriers to prevent moisture from entering the walls. However, throughout most of the continent, natural climatic conditions are complex and miscalculations in the application of this "non-breathable" approach to construction has resulted in accelerating the process that it was meant to avoid. Moisture trapped within walls by plastic barriers has resulted in countless building failures, causing moldy and unhealthy indoor air.

Massive breathable or "flow through" wall construction such as clay/straw, eliminates indoor air-quality problems associated with the trapping of moisture through the wall. Airborne moisture is intercepted by clay in the first inch or two of the wall long before it reaches the wall's dew point or condensation zone. In a temperate climate, using solid-mass walls is a good starting point for a healthy home.

AVOIDING CHEMICAL SOUP

With a healthy wall system in place, the next step is to avoid using toxic substances *inside* the home because they are harmful to health...of factory workers and the environment where toxins are manufactured, of construction workers when they are applying these materials, and of the occupants who will breathe in fumes from construction materials for months and even years after moving in. This fact seems so obvious that it is hard to believe that avoiding toxins is not simply a matter of standard practice. Sadly, however, it is not.

Although the U.S. Environmental Protection Agency (EPA) has stated that "indoor air pollution in residences, offices, schools, and other buildings is widely recognized as one of the most serious potential environmental risks to human health" (1997 Budget Report, p. 47) they have not been as effective in protecting us as one might hope or imagine.

According to a recent study by The Environmental Working Group, "U.S. chemical companies hold licenses to make 75,000 chemicals for commercial use."(*Body Burden,* Environmental Working Group study, January 2003, p. 10). How much do we really know about the health effects of these chemicals? The chilling reality as explained by the Environmental Working Group, is that

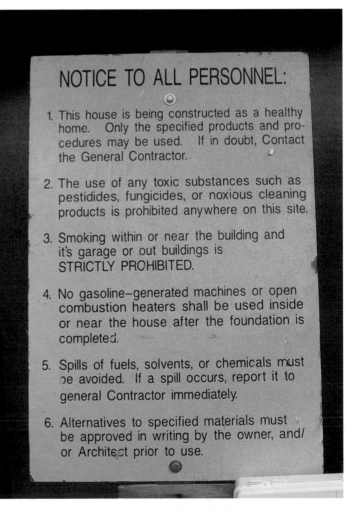

A job-site sign educates newcomers that this is a healthy house.

"for chemicals that are already on the market, the EPA can request data only when it can substantiate that the chemical is causing harm, which it generally cannot do without the toxicity data it is seeking to request... Fewer than half of the applications to the EPA for new chemical production include any toxicity data at all... When data are provided they are typically cursory in nature and the government lacks authority to request anything more than that. Eight of ten new chemicals win approval in less than three weeks, at an average rate of seven a day." (Environmental Working Group Web site, www.ewg. org/reports/bodyburden/factsheets/welltested.php.)

Furthermore, the use of chemicals known to be harmful is rarely restricted. Often, our only protection is the warning labels on the containers. Reading product labels or studying the material safety data sheets of common finishing products, one quickly discovers that many of the products going into our homes can cause a myriad of adverse medical conditions, including respiratory damage, chronic dermatitis, central nervous system damage, and multiple chemical sensitivities. Suspected and known human carcinogens are also in common use in the construction of the standard home. The cumulative and synergistic effects of several chemicals interacting at the same time in an environment have never been adequately studied, and yet that "new home smell" that we are all familiar with in standard construction is the aroma of chemical soup!

There is nothing complicated about building healthier homes. However, building for health is not the criterion for materials choice or building practices in standard housing today. Fortunately, since better materials exist, it is just a matter of seeking them out and making sure that they are used in the construction. We have done this by creating a specification manual for each econest that includes healthy materials choices and procedures and a resource guide so that materials can be easily found. Nature provides a treasure trove of beautiful, sustainable and healthy building materials and we rely heavily upon this abundant source. Several of the books listed in the Resources section of this book contain detailed information about healthier choices.

We find that our econest clients are often savvy about eating healthy foods, drinking clean water, caring for their bodies, and consuming with conscious restraint to preserve precious natural resources. For many, their home is the all-important missing piece in their quest for holistic living. Once they are educated about the dangers found in many building products they become committed partners in making wise choices for what goes into their homes. For them, building an econest is a natural extension of their commitment to an environmentally sound and healthy lifestyle.

DESIGNING FOR HEALTH

Beyond creating a healthy wall system and choosing safe materials, there are several design features that help to promote health, and we incorporate them into econest design. These include:

- SEPARATING THE LIVING SPACE FROM CAR FUMES. The attached garage is often a major source of pollution within the home, especially when the separation walls and doors are not airtight, when the garage is not vented separately, and when the occupants run the car in the garage.

- CREATING A SPACE TO TAKE SHOES OFF AT THE FRONT DOOR. Dirt, dust, pollen, and pesticides tracked in on shoes are best left at the door. It is much easier to keep a home clean and sanitary when the source of pollution is eliminated. The home design can make the shoe-removal habit easy by simply placing the entry a step below the rest of the home, providing a space to sit and remove shoes and a place to store them.

- INCLUDING ACCESSIBLE AND APPEALING OUTDOOR SPACES TO FACILITATE A CONNECTION WITH NATURE AND ITS RHYTHMS. Much has been written about the restorative properties of nature. Fresh air, soothing sounds, and vibrant color are a welcome contrast to workdays spent in front of computer screens and in conditioned spaces. The average person spends in excess of 90 percent of his or her time indoors. By creating easily accessible and beautiful outdoor spaces, a good design can invite us to enjoy time in pleasant and nurturing outdoor surroundings.

- PROVIDING PROPER VENTILATION. Both mechanical and natural ventilation are desirable to evacuate moisture and other occupant-generated pollution. In locations where outdoor conditions are not always optimal, providing a mechanical system to bring in filtered and tempered outside air ensures high-quality indoor air year-round.

- PLANNING AND DESIGNING A HOUSE LAYOUT FOR SAFE ELECTRICAL INSTALLATIONS. Many reports and studies have pointed to the dangers of man-made electromagnetic fields. There are several simple precautions that can be incorporated into any construction to avoid excessive exposure in our homes. These include using metal cable or conduit to shield out electric fields, placing bedrooms away from appliances like computers and refrigerators that generate magnetic fields, and carefully directing wiring raceways away from living areas.

- INCLUDING DRAINS WHERE A WATER SOURCE MIGHT LEAK AND CAUSE DAMAGE, such as in a laundry room. Although this is a simple precaution that can prevent severe damage and health-threatening mold conditions, floor drains, where not required by code, are often overlooked in standard construction.

- SEPARATING THE LIVING SPACE FROM BY-PRODUCTS OF COMBUSTION. Serious illness, chronic ill health, and even death can result from exposure to by-products of combustion from home heating appliances. This damage can easily be avoided. In the econest we isolate the mechanical room from the living space to provide combustion safety and eliminate any noise pollution associated with the mechanical system.

COMBINING HEALTH AND ECOLOGY

"Bau-biologie," or building biology, is a household word throughout much of northern Europe and is the kernel from which the green building movement in Europe sprang. The econest embraces the philosophy of Bau-biologie.

"There is almost always a direct correlation between the biological compatibility of a given material and its ecological performance" (quoted from the online study course by IBE, Clearwater, Florida, www.buildingbiology.net). This one statement embodies the essence of Bau-biologie, a holistic approach to the science of building first formulated in the 1970s by founder Dr. Anton Schneider of Neubeuern, Germany.

In fact, there are twenty-five principles for creating healthy environments that are the basis of Bau-biologie. These embrace many disciplines, including architecture, city planning, engineering, biology, medicine, sacred geometry, and psychology. Combined, they help us strive for a holistic understanding of the complex relationship between human health, the built environment, and the natural world.

Several of these principles deal with the spiritual, psychological, and subtle physical factors that contribute to our sense of well-being. They include the following:

The entrance at Dr. Anton Schneider's Institute for Bau-biologie in Germany.

- ◉ CONSIDERATION OF THE SITE GEOBIOLOGY AND THE PRESERVATION OF NATURAL MAGNETIC FIELDS
- ◉ INCORPORATION OF NATURAL LIGHT, ILLUMINATION, AND COLOR
- ◉ ARCHITECTURAL PROPORTIONING AND THE HARMONIC ORDER OF SPACE
- ◉ THE MINIMIZATION OF MAN-MADE ELECTROMAGNETIC FIELDS
- ◉ ACOUSTICAL PROTECTION FROM NOISE POLLUTION
- ◉ RESPECT FOR THE SOCIOLOGICAL STRUCTURES OF FAMILY AND THE LARGER COMMUNITY

Other principles of Bau-biologie address the issues of environmental health on a global scale. These considerations include:

- ◉ THE USE OF NATURAL AND LOCAL MATERIALS THAT ARE RENEWABLE AND LOW IN EMBODIED ENERGY

- THE USE OF ENERGY-EFFICIENT MATERIALS AND BUILDING SYSTEMS
- THE AVOIDANCE OF MATERIALS WHOSE PRODUCTION EXPLOITS OTHER HUMAN BEINGS OR THE ENVIRONMENT
- THE EMPLOYMENT OF SOLAR ENERGY AND RADIANT HEAT SOURCES

There are sixteen criteria for the selection of building materials. Some of these are not promoted or even discussed in the current mainstream practice of ecological building in North America but are central from a Bau-biologie perspective. These include: history of performance, natural occurrence, thermal properties, absence of radioactivity, diffusion, hygroscopicity, and acoustical properties. Once considered, they make a strong argument for the use of clay, straw, stone, and wood for the flesh and bones of our homes.

THE ELEMENTS OF ECONEST DESIGN AND CONSTRUCTION

THE TIMBERFRAME STRUCTURE

In North America, timber framing is a revived craft serving today's needs for durable shelter. Timber framing is a specific type of post-and-beam construction in which solid wood timbers are connected by means of traditional wooden joinery. The beauty of a carefully crafted frame nurtures a profound connection to nature, invoking a deep sense of serenity. It has been said, "If you care for your home, the home will care for you." Crafted homes invite our care as they reflect the craftsman's conscious participation. Coveted from generation to generation, timberframe homes enrich the lives of those who live in them.

Wood is a renewable resource provided that it is harvested wisely, used sparingly, and replanted diligently. A timberframe structure that is protected from the elements will remain serviceable for many generations, as is demonstrated by the countless historic examples still in use throughout the world today. By using local woods that are sustainably harvested, and by surrounding the timbers with "outsulating" walls and large roof overhangs, we build econest structures to last. When the serviceable life of a timberframe building is over, the pegged timbers with their mortise-and-tenon joinery can be disassembled and reused elsewhere.

We use two basic styles of timber framing in econest designs, European style and Japanese style. The European style, which is more common in North America than the Japanese style, is characterized by diagonal knee bracing and heavier timbers. More often we use a system of horizontal bracing, sometimes referred to as Japanese bracing. Stylistically, this form of bracing creates quieter lines and contributes to a more serene feel within the home.

When a design calls for a European style of timber frame with diagonal knee braces, we hold the braces in one inch from the perimeter wall to facilitate easy installation and removal of formwork plywood. This allows full sheets of plywood between the back of the brace and the inside face of the matrix, eliminating the need to scribe plywood to fit against curved knee braces. When plywood is stripped it leaves a 3/4-inch gap between the back of the brace and the clay/straw, which allows the plaster to flow behind the brace and avoid a shrinkage opening.

An erected timberframe integrates Japanese and European bracing.

Due to its rectangular configuration the "Japanese" style of timber framing naturally simplifies the clay/straw formwork, resulting in almost all of the form plywood being recyclable for roof sheathing.

It is not unusual for us to combine both Japanese and European styles of timber framing in an econest.

A wedged-through tenon under the top of a tenon post shows two examples of male joinery in a timber frame.

PROTECTION FOR THE NATURAL WALL SYSTEM

"A GOOD HAT AND A GOOD PAIR OF BOOTS"

Clay/straw can withstand getting wet because clay is very effective at wicking any water out of the wall and drying it. However, if impeded from drying, clay/straw will eventually mold and decompose.

There is an adage in old English building lore that, to have a long life, a building must have a "good hat and a good pair of boots." We agree. The typical econest has a four-foot-wide roof overhang to serve as its hat. The clay/straw material begins one foot above standing snow level at any given site. Below the clay/straw, the masonry stem wall is protected by a stone wainscoting. This feature,

like a good pair of boots, keeps the bottom of the clay/straw dry.

In addition, we provide our clay/straw walls with a good breathable overcoat. In the desert Southwest we typically use clay-based plasters. In wetter climates with more than twenty inches of annual rain, we use various wood treatments such as shingles or siding over a ventilated space. Before the wood treatment is applied, an air barrier made of clay is plastered over the clay/straw.

Lime-based plasters are commonly used in damper regions of Europe and are also available in North America.

HEATING, COOLING, AND VENTILATING NATURALLY

Ventilation, shading, mass walls, earth coupling, and direct solar gain are all strategies used in econest design to minimize the need for mechanical heating, cooling, and ventilation.

For an econest, a good hat means a four-foot-wide roof overhang.

Stone wainscoting keeps the bottom of the clay/straw wall dry.

NATURAL VENTILATION

Natural ventilation is achieved by providing operable windows on at least two exterior walls in each living space and from one room through the next within an open floor plan. Large roof overhangs shade the exterior mass walls in the summer when the sun angle is high. This reduces daytime heat buildup on the walls and prevents direct solar gain through the windows.

MASS WALLS

Massive exterior walls create a flywheel effect. The walls slowly cool down at night and slowly heat up during the day with the overall result of moderating the home's internal temperature. We use clay/straw for exterior walls and whenever possible we use adobe (sun-dried mud bricks) coated with a 3/4-inch-thick plaster coating for interior walls. These walls contribute to the overall mass of the building and help create a consistently comfortable indoor environment.

Earth coupling with flagstone and earth floors allows geothermal energy to be a moderating force on temperature.

EARTH COUPLING

Beneath a home the earth remains at a constant temperature of 55 degrees. Earth coupling places a massive floor of clay soil, concrete, or stone in direct contact with the earth. Tapping into the earth allows these floors to absorb and radiate the moderating influence to help cool the interior in the summer and warm it in the winter. With the addition of radiant-heating tubes embedded in the massive floors, very little energy is required to heat an econest, and mechanical cooling is seldom required to maintain a high degree of comfort.

In New Mexico we typically have a diurnal temperature swing of 30 to 40 degrees, but through the use of earth coupling, mass walls, shading, and cross ventilation the internal temperature swing in an econest over the same time period will be less than 10 degrees.

Massive interior adobe walls help moderate an econest's indoor climate.

SOLAR HEATING

Econests are oriented to cardinal directions to take advantage of solar heating in the winter. The "sun bump" is a glazed portion of the south wall that protrudes under the roof so that it allows for solar heat gain in the winter but remains shaded in the summer when the sun is at a higher angle from the horizon.

CREATING COMPACT SPACES

One good way to reduce our consumption of energy and materials is to build as if every inch matters. Open floor plans that incorporate the timber frame as a place-defining element, sliding shoji screens, built-in storage, and extension to outdoor spaces are all strategies that we use in our econest designs to give a feeling of spaciousness that belies their smaller-than-average building footprints.

A sun bump on the outside creates an inviting winter garden on the inside. This makes a great place to bask in the sun on a cold winter day. The winter garden remains pleasantly cool and shaded in the summer.

The timber frame, along with the varied ceiling treatments and heights, helps to create several well-defined places within a larger open space.

BRINGING THE INSIDE OUT AND THE OUTSIDE IN

In the context of each home site, we look for the best opportunities to extend living spaces to the outdoors. Timberframe structures and deep roof overhangs are used in econest designs to create outdoor rooms. These spaces can reduce the need for heated space, provide interest and variety to daily life, and simultaneously foster an intimate and regenerative connection with our natural surroundings.

In the winter months the sun bump can become a winter garden filled with greenery and sunshine, dispelling seasonal gloom and bringing the outside indoors.

An ideal window placement will bring in ample light, frame beautiful views, and allow for natural cross ventilation. Through careful window placement in each space and through the use of skylights and rice-paper diffusing screens, econests are designed so that artificial lighting is not required during the daytime and so the natural light is nonglaring and varied.

A timberframe outdoor room serves as an extension of the living space during warm weather.

WATER MANAGEMENT

Water is a precious resource. We design econests to capture it, use it wisely, and recycle it. The large roof has a secondary function as a rainwater collector. Water is channeled via gutters, downspouts, or rain chains, and piped to cisterns, controlling runoff erosion during storms and providing water for gardens during dry weather. Water-conserving appliances and plumbing fixtures are specified. Where permitted by local building codes, gray water (the water that is discharged from sinks, tubs, showers, and laundry after use) is channeled into underground infiltrators where it constantly recharges the groundwater. This supports plant life, which, in turn, supports the local fauna.

This copper rain chain from Japan directs the water to storage systems as it falls from the eaves.

Workshops

"ENGAGE IN THE PROCESS OF CREATING YOUR HOME"

If you have taken the time and initiative to explore the building alternatives presented in the pages of this book, perhaps it is because you are seeking to build a home that does not yet exist amongst the available real estate offerings.

Imagine entering a comfortable and nurturing home built of natural materials and discovering that the home has supported a continuum of family life for several hundred years! Although a rare scenario in North America, this experience is commonplace for most Europeans and may help to explain their absolute trust and respect for their home-building traditions. The econest building techniques have their roots in these time-tested traditions.

Ironically, these building materials and techniques are just beginning to be appreciated in this young country where industrialized building practices predominate to such an extent that to build traditionally is a pioneering venture. To build such a home is an opportunity to leave behind the standard home-production paradigm and discover the innate natural builder in you! Perhaps you are already a professional builder. Or perhaps you have spent your professional life far removed from the tools of the building trades. Hands-on building of the clay/straw walls is something that anyone can participate in, and we consider attending a workshop to be an essential experience in evaluating these mate-

rials for yourself. Clay, straw, and timber are the tools and the teachers in an econest natural home-building workshop.

Although we have described the basics of clay/straw building, making, moving, and placing thirty tons of material is an exercise in people management and material handling that is best learned hands-on in a workshop. An average-sized econest of approximately 1,400 square feet will require about 60,000 pounds of wet material!

The actual mixing and placing of the clay/straw walls is a process that invites owner and community participation. The creation of these walls is the most labor-intensive part of the construction, but it is these walls that create the distinctive feel of the home. Simple framing and formwork also invite workshop participation, with skilled craftsmen on hand to supervise.

Each workshop brings together a wide variety of participants who have come to learn about the econest building system. Typically the workshops, which are sponsored by the new homeowner-to-be, will attract highly skilled timber framers in search of a natural wall system, professional architects and builders wanting to learn about the econest system for clients, and people exploring the possibilities of building a natural home of their own. Attendees come from all over Canada and the United States and include teenagers to

Students erecting a timberframe in a workshop.

octogenarians from different climates, cultures, and backgrounds. Participants are invited to bring an open mind, a pioneering spirit, and the desire to learn through doing and having fun!

Along with hands-on building experience, we feel that it is most important for any novice natural builder to have a firm understanding of building science as it relates to natural building systems. When you choose to build a natural home, you will value knowing how the building works because natural building, once the only type of building, is now considered experimental throughout most of the country. You may find yourself in the position of spokesperson for a growing ecological building movement, because when you build it, they will come!

To this end, several breaks each day are structured into our workshop schedules to talk about the theory and practice of natural building through questions, answers, and presentations. These include topics such as Bau-biologie, healthy building, and the historic context of timber frames, clay/straw, and plasters. We find that a workshop brings together a wide diversity of expertise, and we try to take advantage of the opportunity. We encourage attendees who have an area of related experience to share with the group. We have had excellent presentations by attendees on various pertinent topics including solar power, water catchment, plumbing, and permaculture, to name a few.

We like to treat our workshop attendees to other aspects of natural healthy living that are harmonious with the work they are immersed in. Nutritious organic meals, yoga, and a trip to a traditional Japanese bathhouse for a hot soak under the stars are all part of the Santa Fe workshop program.

Creating a home from scratch, although one of the most rewarding things a family can do, is a mammoth task! A "meet the owner evening" is an opportunity for attendees to tour completed econests. To help you prepare for the challenging journey of building a home, the homeowners are on hand to share their own building experiences and answer any questions the students may have.

We see the workshop as a multilevel assessment opportunity. It is an opportunity for participants to answer some crucial questions for themselves:

◉ ARE NATURAL MATERIALS THE RIGHT THING FOR ME?

◉ IS THIS PARTICULAR SYSTEM THE APPROPRIATE BUILDING RESPONSE FOR MY LOCATION?

◉ WHAT WILL IT TAKE TO GET THIS THROUGH MY BUILDING DEPARTMENT?

◉ HOW SKILLED IS THE INNATE BUILDER IN ME?

◉ IS BECOMING AN OWNER/BUILDER REALISTIC AT THIS TIME OR AM I GOING TO NEED TO MUSTER MORE RESOURCES OR SKILLS BEFORE EMBARKING ON MY OWN PROJECT?

Although certain aspects of the art and craft of building can take a lifetime to master, our goal is to equip each participant, whether professional or novice, so that they are empowered and inspired to pursue their natural building goals.

Making It Happen For You

Bureaucratic acceptance of alternative building materials varies from state to state. Natural wall systems are often classified as "experimental" or viewed with suspicion by building officials. Ironically, many fine examples of clay/straw construction dating back eight hundred years remain in use throughout Europe, attesting to the durability of these breathable walls.

In New Mexico, where codes are already in place for adobe and strawbale construction, building non-loadbearing walls that combine the two materials was not a huge leap. State officials were willing to work with us to create a set of official guidelines. (Refer to page 126 for the New Mexico State Guidelines for Clay/Straw Construction.) Several building officials and inspectors also attended a workshop as our guests and got hands-on experience with the materials. We make a point of inviting local code officials to participate or drop by wherever we do a workshop because we feel that it is an opportunity for them to become familiar with these natural building techniques. This familiarity will perhaps in turn help pave the way towards acceptance for others who wish to build using traditional materials.

For anyone considering building with clay/straw, preliminary discussions with the local building officials are in order. These officials have the jurisdiction and ability to approve or reject your project. Most manufactured building products undergo standardized and very costly testing procedures by nationally recognized testing labs. If they meet certain parameters they are approved automatically and officials do not question their use. This is not the case with nonproprietary, naturally occurring building materials such as clay and straw, so special permission may be required from local building departments. It is important to do your homework in advance and then approach the building officials with respect. Be ready to hear their concerns and answer their questions. The New Mexico State Guidelines, photographs of successful projects in neighboring jurisdictions, a copy of this book, letters from other code officials, and copies of test results from Canada and the United States are all good materials to have on hand at the preliminary meeting.

EIGHT COMMON QUESTIONS ABOUT ECONESTS

1. HOW MUCH WILL AN ECONEST COST TO BUILD?

An econest is an heirloom-quality home built to last for centuries. A handcrafted home always costs more than a standard production home. Though prices vary from region to region, the cost of an econest will be comparable to other high-quality custom homes in your region. Good design can help you to plan a slightly smaller, more efficient home so that more money is available to spend on quality materials. Although initial costs are higher than for most production housing, the savings begin the day the first utility bills arrive. The compact space, energy-efficient wall system, ample daylight, and passive solar design will result in lower energy costs throughout the long life of the home.

2. IS CLAY/STRAW WALL CONSTRUCTION SUITABLE FOR EVERY CLIMATE?

Because an econest has both mass storage and insulative properties, it is well suited for temperate climates that experience both hot summers and cold winters. The clay/straw walls must thoroughly dry before the application of finish materials such as plaster or wood siding. For 12-inch-thick walls we recommend that construction be timed so that there is a predictable three-month dry season while the clay/straw is curing. The occasional rain during this time will not adversely affect the process. Econests have proven to be a durable solution for a range of diverse climates from Iowa and Wisconsin to New Mexico and Colorado. Clay/straw is not a good choice for areas without clay, and areas that do not have a dependable dry season. It is also not a good choice for tropical climates that do not require insulation, or climates with several feet of standing snow.

3. IS THERE A BUILDER IN MY AREA WHO KNOWS HOW TO BUILD WITH CLAY/STRAW?

If you wish to build with this system and don't have a trained builder in your area, find a builder who is willing to learn and bring him or her with you to a workshop. In the Resources we have listed some clay/straw builders who have been trained in our system.

4. WHERE IS THE VAPOR BARRIER IN A CLAY/STRAW WALL?

No vapor barrier is necessary in a 12-inch-thick clay/straw wall. Clay has the ability to hold many times its weight in moisture without deteriorating. It has the ability to wick water away from wood and straw, and to release the moisture back into the air when the ambient air humidity drops. The clay itself acts as a huge network to intercept, hold, and then release moisture in the first couple of inches of the wall so that no significant amount of moisture ever penetrates to the dew-point zone. Because of this, a vapor barrier is not required and in fact would be detrimental to the wall because it would trap moisture, setting up conditions for decay.

5. WILL CLAY/STRAW BE APPROVED BY OUR BUILDING DEPARTMENT?

Clay/straw has already been approved in many building departments throughout the world. Building codes in the United States have a provision for alternative methods and building materials. It is left up to the discretion of the building official as to whether or not you will be granted a permit. Clay/straw is a relatively new building system in this country and your building department may be unfamiliar with it. The official New Mexico guidelines found on page 126 may be a helpful document when presenting your case to your local official. Be knowledgeable, be prepared listen to your official's concerns, and be respectful.

6. CAN WE GET A MORTGAGE FOR THIS BUILDING SYSTEM?

Several of the econests that we have built carry conventional mortgages. Because most lenders are familiar with timberframe structures and because the clay/straw is non-loadbearing, there is usually not a problem. However, we urge you to speak with your lender early on in the planning stages.

7. WHAT ABOUT MOLD?

All straw contains mold, as does any other plant material. Mold will also rapidly appear on any industrialized building product with cellulose in it whenever atmospheric conditions are favorable to mold growth. Gypsum board (also known as wallboard or drywall), the most common interior wall surface in standard construction, contains cellulose in the form of recycled newsprint. All wood is composed of cellulose, as well. If exposed to certain conditions these materials will become moldy within a few hours. This is because they provide food for ever-present airborne mold to colonize on. When the clay/straw mixture is wet, dormant mold spores will become activated. We add borax to the water to retard this process. However, there may be some mold present on the drying surfaces. This is normal.

Once the walls are dried and plastered, air-quality tests have shown that there are no elevated indoor mold counts. In fact, the mold counts are lower than those found outdoors, which is what one would expect to find in a healthy house. Occasional wetting of the plaster will not cause mold growth because of the exceptional ability of clay to wick water away from the straw and re-release it into the air. This is why throughout history mankind has successfully used clay as a natural preservative. The key to a mold-free home, whether it be of clay/straw or standard construction, is to have good construction, which prevents water intrusion; good ventilation, which prevents the buildup of humidity created by human activity; and good maintenance, so that any water leakage is detected and repaired before it becomes problematic.

8. IS IT IMPORTANT TO ATTEND A WORKSHOP?

Until very recent history, natural homes were the only type of homes available. However, if you are considering building a natural home today, you are an ecological pioneer and you will find yourself becoming a spokesperson for the burgeoning natural building movement by your example. This decision is not for everyone and we feel strongly that it is important to be well educated and articulate about your choices. There are several different systems for building with natural materials, including straw bale, cob, and adobe, and you may wish to attend a variety of workshops before deciding which system makes the most sense for you. The workshop provides a fertile meeting ground for like-minded people from across the continent. There is often an opportunity to experience finished homes and meet and interview people who have already been through the process. It is also a time to learn by doing. See if these materials speak to you loud enough for you to be able to speak for them, because if you build this way, people will come.

Case

Studies

A MIDWEST NEST

PROJECT: Connet Residence, formerly Robert Laporte's Residence

DESIGNER: Robert Laporte

BUILDER: Robert Laporte

LOCATION: Fairfield, Iowa

No Waste, No Pollution. "This first econest was the end product of a long journey and the departure point for a new one which I find myself in the midst of today, nearly fifteen years later. In 1989 I was deeply inspired to build a home following the regenerative example of nature—without waste and without pollution. I came across a picture of an Eskimo building an igloo in the Arctic. I said to myself, 'If this person can build a shelter using only a whale bone and frozen water, then I must be sitting on a gold mine here in the Midwest!' In fact, like the Eskimo, every preindustrial culture had evolved a system for creating homes using the local natural materials. My research led me to Europe where timber frames, still in use, predated both the industrial revolution and the panelized wall systems that are most commonly used in modern-day timber framing as practiced in North America. In Germany I was introduced to clay/straw walls, clay plasters, and an active ecological building movement

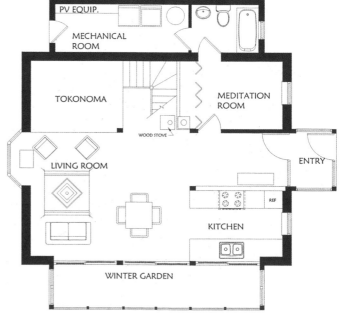

FIRST FLOOR

SECOND FLOOR

This view of the southwest corner shows the simplicity of the two-story structure, whose roof extends to create the solar greenhouse. Below the double skylights there is a glimpse of the photovoltaic array, placed on the south face of the roof for maximum exposure. At the peak, the "Boston ridge" moderates the interior climate by siphoning hot air from the roof cavity and keeping the insulation cooler. In the summer, an interior ceiling exhaust vent at the apex is opened and draws rising hot air out of the building through the Boston ridge, passively creating a cooling airflow. Note the four-foot roof overhangs and the west balcony, which shade the walls and windows from summer sun. In response to the Midwest's climate with its frequent driving rains, durable cedar siding was chosen to protect the clay/straw walls. Lime plaster would also be an appropriate choice in this wet region.

Kitchen cabinetry boxes and door frames were handmade of solid cedar. For contrast, strips of fir were thinly sliced and woven to adorn the door fronts and ventilate the cabinets. This creative door design was an innovation of Duncan McMaster, a local master craftsman who also made the original shoji screens for the house. A light-colored limestone countertop, oiled and sealed with plant-based products, was quarried from Stone City, Iowa, sixty miles away. The same limestone slabs over a radiant-heated earth sub-base were used on the ground-level floors, creating a naturally comfortable heat sink. This was the first econest application of an earth-coupled floor.

"A nest is a cup of space, a swinging cradle, an anchored platform, a wedge between boulders, a pocket in bark or dirt, a scrape on rock, a dent in sand. It represents the still point in a bird's fast-paced life, the place where past and future meet."

— GRETEL EHRLICH, FOREWORD TO *The Nest*

based on the use of natural materials. On my return to Iowa I set out to create a prototype that showcased these techniques, in which the entire home would have the same soulful presence as the timber frame.

"The home was designed to demonstrate the following features:

◉ RENEWABLE ENERGY

◉ WASTE RECYCLING

◉ WATER CATCHMENT

◉ NATURAL BUILDING

◉ NATURAL HEATING, COOLING, AND VENTILATION

John and Carole Connet in front of their Iowa econest. A fence encircles the home according to the Vedic building principles known as *vastu*. The Connets chose durable bamboo and cedar for their fence. In the space above the entry, formerly a balcony, John and Carole added a studio finished with cedar shakes and siding to match the original home.

By the time the clay/straw was under way, the project was a curiosity far and wide. It seemed as though a common chord had been struck, bringing reporters and other people from all over the country.

"I knew I had passed my final inspection when, while meditating upstairs in the west wing one day, I was stirred to open my eyes only to find a wild rabbit sitting outside the east entrance. After a moment and much to my surprise, that rab-

bit jumped onto the threshold as I held my breath in utter amazement. He stepped inside, took a look around, then began to nibble on a nearby mat while he made himself at home. This was significant. A wild rabbit would shun most man-made environments. I had created a shelter so akin to the surrounding natural one that even a rabbit felt welcome."

— Robert Laporte

Finding our Dream Home.

"Our house is a cup of space floating on a platform of gravel, wedged between limestone blocks. It is built of mud and straw like the barn swallow's nest, plastered between white pine posts and beams, joined together with wooden pegs. It is squared off at the corners, not rounded, like a unique, handmade Japanese tea-ceremony cup. The inside is lined with white mulberry paper, goose-down pillows, and Persian and Tibetan rugs. Many people built our nest, toting buckets of red clay mud mixed with wheat straw and tramping the mixture between wooden forms. I added the lining. Our econest provides the still point in our fast-paced life. We begin each day in a quiet bath of stillness, and we end each day surrounded by a fluffy comforter of tranquility.

"The first time I saw our nest-to-be, it was love at first breath. My friend Carolyn Sims brought me out to see Robert's first clay/straw timberframe construction not long after the walls had been raised by the loving labor of many, many hands and feet. We walked through the open front door into a vessel of sunlight, fresh straw, damp clay, and silence thick as honey. I stood on the earthen floor in the middle of all that light and space, like a weary traveler soaking in a warm tub. Turning to Carolyn I said, 'Someday I'm going to live in a house like this,' little knowing how, as a single mother, that would ever come to pass, and never dreaming it would be this very house. Six years later when John, my new spouse, and I told Carolyn, now a realtor, we were looking for our dream house, she took us out to see Robert's original home, on the market for the first time since he had moved to New Mexico. The moment I stepped through the front door, I breathed a long-held 'Aaah.' The house, now finished and furnished, greeted me with the same deep, dynamic silence. The finishing touches of white shoji screens; limestone flagstones; and hand-planed, silken woodwork only added to my growing love affair.

"Like a bird's nest, our house came together from many natural sources. The clay was dug on-site, the straw locally grown, the white pine salvaged from nearby highway construction, the limestone quarried at Stone City, Iowa. The 12-inch-thick clay/straw walls breathe, as does the cedar-shake roof with its cotton insulation. The mortise-and-tenon construction withstood a 100 mph wind that felled an 80-foot shagbark hickory, which, when it landed on our small timberframe shed, only knocked off a few shingles. From my crow's nest upstairs, I could see the trees bent sideways and hear the roar

The Connets' delicate pottery collection is nestled solidly in this pegged wooden assembly. This joint, with a hidden spline, was handcrafted using a Japanese joinery technique. Not visible in the photo is the beam extending beyond to support the balcony.

of the wind, but the house didn't budge an inch. I felt completely safe.

"Part of the magic of this house is built into the design, which is based on the ancient Vedic principles of *vastu*, or proper placement. The front doors face east to catch the daily renewal of light, which passes straight through the house. All the doors are glass, allowing light from windows and skylights to pass from one side to the other through the open center of the house, called the *brahmastan*. A low, bamboo fence defines the *vastu* perimeter of the house. To me it feels like being nestled in the fork of an ancient oak.

"Soon after we moved in, four moving men struggled to carry a gigantic pine wardrobe through the front door and across the flagstones to the pine platform at the foot of the stairs. They gently set their burden down and centered it against the clay-plaster wall. Then they stood back, wiping sweat from their foreheads with their shirtsleeves. One of them handed me the invoice. But they didn't make a move to leave, just stood around in their jeans and farmer's caps, gazing out the bay window and up at the pine ceiling, not saying a word. I offered them some lemonade. The invoice man found his voice. 'It sure feels different in here,' he said. This scene repeats itself every time visitors enter our econest; within moments, the magic overtakes them. They fall silent. Finally one will say, 'It's so quiet here.' They sit. They gaze out the sunroom windows, reluctant to leave.

"And so it is with us. We sit around the table. The sun shines through the many windows. We linger long after meals, not speaking. Sometimes we read a book or wash the dishes. John fixes a broken clock or repairs a reed organ. I play my flute, write a poem, or paint, creating something from the materials of myself in a beautiful nest that protects the spirit."

— Carole Connet

Retractable shoji panels and privacy screens, a sisal rug, and a textured spruce ceiling with a rice-paper lantern greet visitors as they enter the house, a world apart from the surrounding Iowa cornfields.

This west-facing bay window is flanked by timberframe posts that carry a Japanese brace above. Carole's plate collection is displayed on the brace. To the right, a Japanese lantern and colorful kimono capture the flavor of the "Tokanoma," or "raised beauty," corner derived from Japanese architecture. The beautiful earth-tone hue of the walls is the natural color of the plaster made from clay harvested on-site.

OPPOSITE » Open, cedar shelving and deep windowsills provide display space for the Connets' tableware, which is too pretty to hide behind doors.

AN ACTIVIST DEMONSTRATES

PROJECT: Lynne McGee Residences

ARCHITECT: Baker-Laporte and Associates

BUILDER: Lynne McGee, owner/builder, and Econest Building Company

LOCATION: Durango, Colorado, then Bayfield, Colorado

Lynne wanted a home that was compact and open. The resulting design is a 1,100-square-foot, one-and-a-half-story timber frame with utilities and an open living room, dining room, and kitchen on the ground floor. Two open bedrooms are tucked away upstairs under a simple gable roof. The central core of the building is left open with the upstairs spaces overlooking the dining area. The stair wraps around the fire source (a wood-burning stove in her first house and a sculpted fireplace in her second). A timberframed entry porch extends along the face of the building, providing a sheltered outdoor space from which to enjoy a garden view. When Lynne decided to move from Durango to a co-housing community in Bayfield, Colorado, she decided to build the same house again. The only big change she made to her home was the location of the solar bump-out. Her original home entered from the east, so the solar bump-out was located off the dining area. Her new site called for a north entry, so the solar bump was moved to be off the living room that was now oriented to the south. The bump-out on the east remained to capture the morning sun and bring it into the home. According to Lynne, the east bump-out really assists the solar heating during the swing seasons by capturing the morning heat.

A Model of Beautiful Simplicity.
"Our homes, like our food, should support our well-being. To this end, in the early 1990s I renovated several small homes in Boulder, Colorado, using healthy, nontoxic materials to demonstrate that it could be done for less than 10 percent more than the cost of standard procedures. Tours were arranged so that people could experience the differences, and labels throughout explained the various products and criteria for their choices. In addition to being desirable and healthy, environmentally sound homes proved to be highly marketable.

"I had heard of Robert's work and the natural building workshops that he gave for owner/builders, so when the time came to build my own home from scratch I went off to an econest workshop in Santa Fe. By the end of it I had committed to hosting the next workshop, which would be on my land near Durango.

"I wanted my new home to be a model of beautiful simplicity, of space efficiency, energy conservation, and the use

In Lynne's second home, the gable and entry porch are oriented to the north with a pathway and colorful native garden leading to the pedestrian walkway joining her home with the rest of the community.

FIRST FLOOR

ENTRY PORTAL

BATH

ENTRY

KITCHEN

CLOSET #1

MECH./STORAGE

DINING ROOM

LIVING ROOM

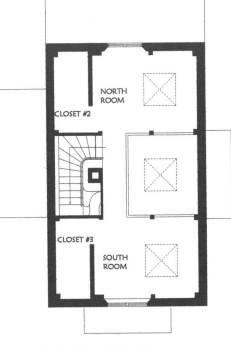

SECOND FLOOR

NORTH ROOM

CLOSET #2

CLOSET #3

SOUTH ROOM

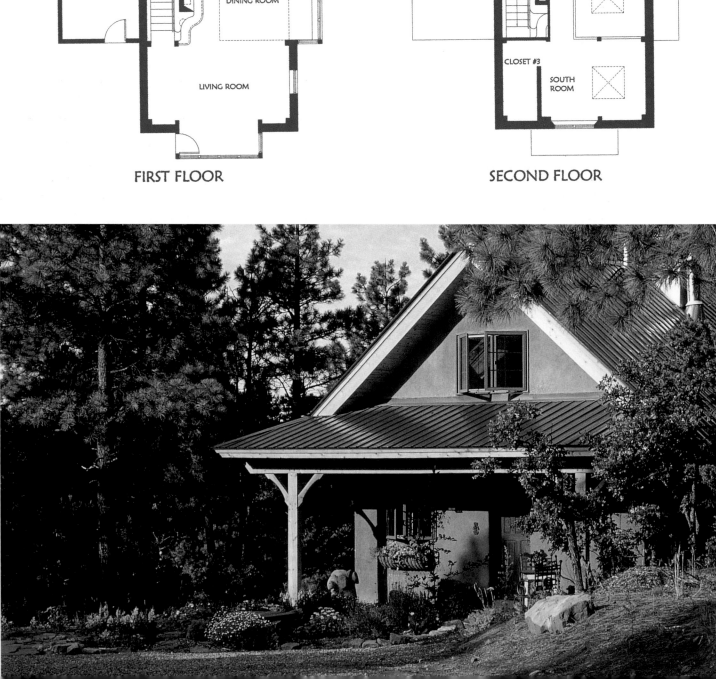

LEFT » With light streaming through the skylight, views to nature surrounding the table, and with earth underfoot, eating here is like the finest alfresco dining.

BELOW » With a fanciful spice rack and pot hanger for storage, windows may take the space upper cabinets usually fill. The galley kitchen is a statement in efficiency with everything needed at arm's reach. Twin counters—one a butcher block, the other stone—meet the needs of chef McGee.

OPPOSITE » Lynne's first home is oriented with the entry portal to the east. The home is tucked into a pine-covered southern slope. A timber frame with curved braces supports the porch roof, creating an outdoor space while protecting the natural wall system.

Lynne in the shade of her covered entry.

of natural materials. Clay/straw provided the balance of mass and insulation so important in a passive solar home in this region. It also had the breathability that, for me, is synonymous with 'aliveness.' As for the timber frame, well, it is just elegant evidence of what holds up the house!

"For some years I had been working with a group of people in planning a co-housing community. A number of these folks had become dear friends in the process. Things were slow to materialize, so when I decided to move forward on a home for myself many of my friends joined me for the workshop. We worked together on the clay/straw walls through a rainy and very muddy workshop in the spring of 1997.

No sooner did I finish my new home than the co-housing community became a reality. Four of the families who helped with my home chose to build in the same way in the Heartwood co-housing community. And I began to contemplate doing it all over again! Once again, contrary to conventional real-estate wisdom about what the market requires, my tiny two-bedroom/single-bath econest sold effortlessly.

"The first home was a delight to live in and I was hard pressed to make changes in building the second time. We added twelve inches to the length of the building, which gave us room for a more luxurious bath and a little extra space in living room. Instead of a central wood-burning stove, I created a sculptural Rumford fireplace that added more mass to the interior and is the central feature of the home. In my new home the mechanical room and storage are in an unheated shed tucked under the extended roof on the west side. Why use heated space to store things? I also removed the storage closet from the loft bedroom. I knew from experience that I wouldn't need it and I preferred the symmetry of the space without it. I work hard at not accumulating 'stuff' and I like an uncluttered look.

"The biggest difference between the two homes is the degree to which I have personalized the second one. This has happened, not as a conscious decision but more as the result of a feeling that, here at the co-housing, I was finally home! I acted on this feeling, albeit unconsciously, when I chose to

A truth window opens to reveal the clay/straw wall concealed beneath layers of clay plaster throughout the rest of the home.

Clay/straw lends itself to sculptural shaping when wet. Here, Lynne has inset a round window framed with one of her treasures, an antique iron grinding wheel.

Gable windows and large skylights give a warm glow to the loft spaces tucked under the steep roof. Although completely open to the rest of the house, the bedroom is defined by the timber frame, with the bed nestled between a pair of queen posts. In the foreground, a timber bridge connects the two upstairs rooms and overlooks the dining room below.

embed personally meaningful objects into the very fabric of my new home. The grinding wheel that I used for a round window frame is an example of this, as are the mosaics and tool-laden railings.

"My home is like a greenhouse in many ways. In the winter the south and east sun bumps are filled with flowers, and the pools of light created by these windows and the skylights bring the outside in at all times of the day. The whole house is heated with a thirty-gallon water heater, and costs me well under two hundred dollars a year to heat. The heat rises by convection to heat the second floor and the excess is vented out through skylights.

"My advice to those who are contemplating building their own home is: do it! I would do it again in a heartbeat. It was a joyful experience for me, primarily because of the people I chose to work with. Those choices make the difference between a nightmare and a great experience. Work with people who share your values and your vision, and get involved in the process yourself. Watching your house evolve into your home through the dance of creativity and hard work is a thrill not to be missed."

— Lynn McGee

This view in Lynne's first house, from the bridge to the dining room below, shows off the home's earthen floors.

BELOW AND RIGHT » An antique pie cabinet built into the wall, a collection of old-fashioned farm implements embedded in the balcony rail, and a collage of tiles and textures set into the dining side of the cabinets reveal the playful soul of artist McGee.

ABOVE » A couch sits in the living room's solar alcove, surrounded by plants. The dropped-beam ceiling provides a cozy contrast to the vaulted dining area. The armoire is one of several throughout the home. Lynne prefers them over conventional closets, which would hide some of the timber frame. Note the transition between tile and earthen floors. Lynne used slate for circulation paths and the softer earth floors for ground-floor living areas.

The banco invites one to melt into the soft curves and warmth of the fireplace, while a stairway wraps around the chimney, beckoning to the loft.

ORGANIC COUNTRY

PROJECT: Daryl Stanton Residence

ARCHITECT: Baker-Laporte and Associates

BUILDER: Econest Building Company, Robert Laporte, and Steve Vessey

LOCATION: La Barbaria Canyon, New Mexico

This home site was a challenging but beautiful one. Located on a narrow strip of land in a box canyon, the building pad sits between a steep hill rising to the west and a sharp drop-off into a grass wetlands to the east. The European style of timber frame was designed in response to the owner's desire for a cozy "country cottage" feel. The 1,700-square-foot main house has an east-entry porch that leads to a solar atrium, then steps up into the central kitchen/dining/living

space. A dense clay/straw wall serves as a heat sink to gently distribute the solar heat between the atrium and the living space. A small wing steps up to the north of the main living space where Daryl's daughter, Brianna, has a study area, bathroom, and bedroom with a play loft. The second-floor master suite tucks under the roof with east-facing gable-end windows facing a dramatic mountain view. A shed dormer expands the upper living space.

In Harmony with Nature.

"I came into the designing and building of my new home with some experience. I had done an extensive remodeling and redecorating of my home in the early '80s and become extremely sick as a result of the chemical exposure. Later I built a healthy home for myself; however, it wasn't particularly ecological. When I came to Robert and Paula, I was interested in building a home that was both healthy for me and the planet. I experienced one of their homes and found it to have a feeling of living in harmony with the land...it smelled like being out in nature, it breathed. It had a feeling unlike any other type of home I had ever been in.

"I wanted a home that had a cozy, organic country feel. Nothing too polished. So the idea of a European-style timber frame with exposed beams, plaster walls, and floors from local earth really appealed to me. I created a country kitchen

and dining area with hanging pots and pans and open shelving for the dishes. Robert and Steve built the cabinetry with solid wood boxes and rough-sawn pine facing. Finding chemical-free furnishings for my new home was a challenge but one that I enjoyed. In fact, when I completed my new home I decided to start a business to help other people create healthy and beautiful interiors, too, and that is how my business, Casa Natura, was born!"

— Daryl Stanton

This view from the southeast shows the south-facing entry solarium with its overhead skylights. The economical story-and-a-half design provides second-floor living under the steep roof, expanded through the use of a shed dormer. The lower portions of the walls at the tall gable end are protected and shaded by a secondary roof.

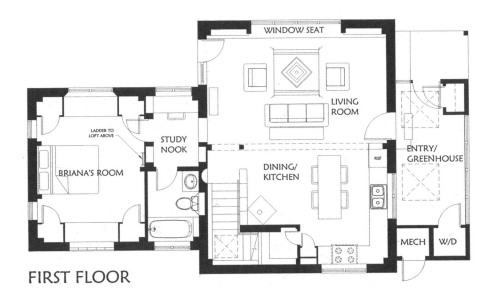

FIRST FLOOR   SECOND FLOOR

Floor plan labels, first floor:
WINDOW SEAT
LIVING ROOM
STUDY NOOK
LADDER TO LOFT ABOVE
BRIANA'S ROOM
DINING/KITCHEN
REF
ENTRY/GREENHOUSE
MECH W/D

Floor plan labels, second floor:
DARYL'S ROOM

The L-shaped footprint creates a sheltered east-facing alcove accessed through a pair of french doors in the living room. The steep metal roof is a good strategy for mountain climates with heavier snowfalls.

BELOW » Daryl, lying in an organic bed, on organic sheets, surrounded by hard-to-find organic baby clothes—all for sale in her store, Casa Natura.

ABOVE » Peaceful quiet is a characteristic quality achieved with 12-inch-thick clay/straw walls. In this bedroom window the massive nature of the wall is revealed by its deep wooden sill, beveled sides, and timber posts.

RIGHT » Interior adobe walls, with their low embodied energy, can add thousands of pounds of mass to the home, an effective natural strategy for moderating indoor climate. A modern-day practice of stabilizing the adobe bricks with asphalt is one that we don't subscribe to. We use only unstabi-lized, or additive-free, sun-dried adobes in our homes to safeguard the health of the occupants.

LEFT » A pair of knee braces creates an archway to the entry porch, which is tucked under the southeast corner of the roof.

ABOVE » In this sunny living room corner, a timberframe post with two knee braces supports stout bookshelves of matching wood. The cream-colored clay for the finish plaster coat was harvested in nearby Galisteo.

RIGHT » Low-beamed ceilings; rough, troweled plaster; and European-style timber frame complement Daryl's healthy furnishings of solid wood, organic cotton, and wool. Structure and furnishings come together to create the old-world feel of her home. A pair of timber posts frame a window seat to the east, completing the seating arrangement.

ABOVE » Fulfillment in life is rooted in health, and there is nothing like a good night's sleep to promote this. Here, Daryl pulls out all the stops with her king-sized Samina Sleep System covered in luxurious organic bedding. Within the walls, all electrical wiring is shielded so that the bedroom is free of electromagnetic fields, contributing to a peaceful night's sleep.

Rough-sawn solid pine cabinets, butcher-block countertops with a slate backsplash, and open pine shelving create a rustic setting. Daryl's handmade tableware, hanging pots, and harvest table complete the cottage-like feel of the kitchen. The range could be placed beneath the window because a downdraft ventilation system was used instead of a hood.

INSPIRED BY JAPAN

PROJECT: Robert Laporte and Paula Baker-Laporte Residence #1

ARCHITECT: Baker-Laporte and Associates

BUILDER: Econest Building Company

LOCATION: Tesuque, New Mexico

"The Peregrine" is the name we gave the first "nest" that we designed and built for ourselves. It is named in honor of the bird used by Japanese falconers because the design was inspired by the home-building traditions of Japan, which we both admire. In it we created compact but flexible space by using the timber frame itself as a defining element and by using a series of sliding rice-paper, or shoji, doors to expand or separate the spaces on a daily basis to meet our needs. The home is 1,370 square feet and consists of a central living core, two bedrooms, two baths, a meditation room, and a solar winter garden.

From Workshop to Wedding Vows.

"I first came across Robert Laporte on paper, in 1993. I was reading an article about his building techniques for creating a natural home. At that time I was recovering from a chronic illness caused by exposure to chemicals commonly found in new home construction. My formal architectural education had not included any training about creating buildings that supported health! This important aspect of building was now a major focus for me both personally and professionally. I had become an avid student of Bau-biologie and was searching for ways to apply these principles of building for health and ecology to my life and practice in Santa Fe, New Mexico. It was in this context that I happened upon an article about Robert. His work applied the fundamentals of Bau-biologie to a much greater degree than anything I had read about or witnessed thus far and I was eager to experience this first-hand. I finished the article, picked up the phone, and booked myself into his next workshop, which was to be held in

Crestone, Colorado, the following month. I went away from the workshop inspired by the knowledge that these natural building techniques were doable, beautiful, durable, and practical. I was determined to somehow incorporate them into

A flat building site was carved out of a south-facing slope. Rock terracing was used to soften the slope into a series of planting beds that are fed by gray water from the home. Great care was taken to preserve the piñon tree to the west of the solar bump-out, which prevents overheating from the harsh west sun. A simple, low-sloped, hipped gable roof of green metal and a stone wainscoting anchor the building to the terraced site. Utilities are located in a detached utility room, which is shared by several of the buildings in our compound. The roof of the utility room serves as a terrace off the master suite.

Robert, Paula, and daughter, Sarah Baker, outside their first econest.

my work. What I could never have imagined then was that six years later Robert and I would be standing together saying our wedding vows in front of eighty friends and family members, under an elephant-trunk beam in our own new econest! As the years have passed my health has gone from fragile to healthy to vibrant. The Peregrine has been my sanctuary, a healing environment, a home that we have joyfully shared together and with the hundreds of people who have come to see it."

— Paula Baker-Laporte

A recessed adobe wall captures heat from the Tulikivi, a Finnish masonry oven, on the opposite side. This makes for a warm and inviting wintertime study corner. Handcrafted shelving from the Canadian store Not Just for the Garden and desk by Taos artist Bruce Peterson, complement the surrounding timber frame.

A succession of framed views unfold from the meditation room, through the living room and solar winter garden beyond, past an herb garden on the top terrace, and finally opening to the sweeping panorama of the Tesuque Valley beyond. With shoji screens closed, the living room becomes an intimate, inwardly focused space bathed in diffuse light, entering through the skylights and filtered through the rice-paper panels above.

LEFT » A sunken entryway carries the outside flagstone into the home and defines the area for coat and shoe removal. Removing shoes is a good way to keep the house clean. We are always reminded of that when we see how much dirt collects in the entryway. Rarely do we have to ask people to take off their shoes because as they come in, the request is implicit.

RIGHT » In the corner of the dining room a plastered adobe wall surrounds the Tulikivi. Prior to the advent of central heating, Northern European countries invented ingenious ways to heat themselves comfortably and efficiently with wood fire and mass masonry ovens or fireplaces that stored the heat. The Dutch tiled oven, the Russian fireplace, the German Kacheloffen, and shown here, a corner model of the Tulikivi (Finnish for *firestone*), are all examples of this technology. Radiant heat is one of the healthiest and most comfortable forms of heat. The rapid full combustion and tight-fitting glass door eliminates the pollution often associated with standard wood stoves and fireplaces.

We have found that after a short nightly fire at dinnertime, the 5,000-pound soapstone unit retains its warmth around the clock and the soapstone bench is an invitation to soak it in. The home remains comfortable all winter with a combination of solar gain from the winter garden and heat from the Tulikivi. Radiant in-floor heating is rarely used except in the bathrooms.

ABOVE » The loadbearing timber frame supports the simple hipped-gable roof, defining a perfect square. Non-loadbearing clay/straw walls weave in and out from the timber frame, defining bump-outs on the interior and covered outdoor rooms. Here, a welcoming east entry is sheltered under the roof. According to *vastu,* an east entry in this location is auspicious, and that has been our experience!

ABOVE » Exposed joinery, natural clay plasters, shoji screens, and reed/rice straw tatami mats reveal the care of many hands that went into the making of this meditation room. Also unique to these screens is the bamboo dividing the rice paper. The tatami mats were a wedding present from Robert. Surrounded by bamboo flooring, they are a wonderfully resilient surface for practicing yoga.

BELOW » The living room, defined by four posts, is a square centrally located within a larger perimeter square. In Vedic architecture this central core is the sacred space, or *brahmastan.* We celebrated this with a rice-paper-and-cedar mandala ceiling that brings a soft light into this central core. The elephant-trunk beam, or "taiko" in Japanese, has a story to tell. In traditional Japanese architecture a curvilinear tree crafted into an otherwise regular timber frame is intended as a tribute to nature from whence all life springs. This tree found us in a northern New Mexico forest. Interestingly, once the beam had been painstakingly fashioned into place we pulled out drawings that had been completed months earlier and realized that the curvature of the beam matched that of the drawing to within half an inch! Hidden behind the pair of woven doors is a TV and other electronic equipment.

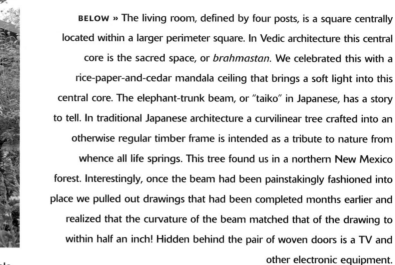

LEFT » The south-facing sun-bump provides for as much as 60 percent of our winter heating needs here in sunny New Mexico. The glazing protrudes to within eighteen inches of the roof overhang and captures winter sun while blocking unwanted summer heat gain. We call this space a winter garden because in the dead of winter it provides a space within the home where we are surrounded by greenery and can bask in the sun, even when outdoor temperatures plummet into single digits. The flagstone floors on gravel act as a good heat sink to store solar heat—and we don't have to worry about spilling water when we water our plants!

RIGHT » This view from the dining room through to the living room and meditation room beyond shows how the various heights and ceiling treatments together with the timberframe compositions define the places within a large, open plan. Visitors are often surprised by the spaciousness when they realize that the home is less than 1,400 square feet. Many clients over the years have downsized their dream homes and opted for quality over quantity as a result of seeing this space.

A Healthy Sanctuary

PROJECT: Michael and Kendal McTeigue Residence

ARCHITECT: Baker-Laporte and Associates with Econest Building Company

TIMBER FRAME AND CLAY/STRAW: Econest Building Company

GENERAL CONTRACTOR: Whole Homes, LLC

LOCATION: Pagosa Springs, Colorado

The McTeigue nest fronts onto a quiet residential street to the north and faces a little lake and open meadow to the south and east. The 1,600-square-foot home has three bedrooms and two baths. The idyllic views of the lake are captured from the master bedroom, dining room, kitchen and portals. The structure is a hybrid combining timber framing in the public central core and Larsen trusses with clay/straw infill for the perimeter walls. Portals surrounding the home are timber frame. A central masonry heater with pizza oven acts as a room divider between the living room and dining areas and is a magnet for family gatherings when the weather turns cold. Large east and west portals expand the family activities to the outdoors and are even used on sunny days throughout the winter in southern Colorado's delightful climate. A detached garage and office help to define an entry courtyard and provide a privacy buffer between the McTeigues and the adjacent home.

A Home that Nurtures Health.

"I own a New York City–based business that allows us to live where we want. My wife, Kendal, and I met in Colorado, but while we lived in New York, we often talked about moving back there to raise our family. Immediately following 9/11 we decided it was time.

"We bought an almost-finished spec home on a beautiful lake in Pagosa Springs, Colorado. We were able to put our personal touches to the home, and we were pleased with the look. However, the day we moved in I became sick and had a cold with symptoms that wouldn't go away. I was sick for the first two weeks of living there. We visited Kendal's mom on two occasions during that time. Each time I began to feel better but as soon as we returned home my symptoms flared up again. We began to realize that our new home might be making me sick. Kendal showed me an article in *Natural Home* magazine about Paula and Robert's method and style of building. That was when we also learned of the phenomenon of 'sick homes' or 'unhealthy houses.' The pieces of my puzzling illness began to fall into place. The article mentioned upcoming econest workshops; we were able to attend one the following week.

An evening view from the lakeshore. The large roof overhang, along with the stone wainscoting, anchors the home to its landscape. The sun bump is stepped forward close to the edge of the roof overhang to collect winter sun, while the master bedroom is recessed, creating a generous shaded outdoor room in the southwest corner, accessible from both the master bedroom and the dining room.

Kendal with Emma, and Michael holding the newest addition, Becky, under the southwest portal overlooking the lake.

"At the workshop Kendal and I learned about the fundamentals and health benefits of econests, and we visited a few. We loved what we saw. We also learned ways to speed up the off-gassing of our new conventionally built home. Over time the chemicals would dispel so that the home would no longer make me sick, but we felt that it would never really nurture our health either. I wasn't willing to compromise my family's health, and mentioned to Paula my desire to provide a healthier, possibly new home for my family. Our conversation suddenly became more animated!

"We owned another lot near our first house and immediately set to planning a new healthy home. Paula and Robert visited and became acquainted with the land, and Paula returned to her studio and began designing. In two months

we were breaking ground. Robert and company came out to Pagosa Springs in July of 2002 to erect the timber frame and clay/straw walls, and then, with the help of an experienced local builder, I took on the rest of the construction myself. As our building progressed Kendal became pregnant with our second child. All through the winter of 2003 the question loomed: Which would arrive first—our new child or our move-in date?

"Rebecca Isabel McTeigue was born on May 10th. We moved into our new home on July 1st. Kendal and I are very pleased with our home. It is one of the nicest homes we've ever been in. Visitors often confirm this. Homes somehow reflect who we are and I feel our home reflects our values in so many ways.

Off the kitchen in this sheltered eastside portal, the morning sun and comfortable furnishings create a warm spot for enjoying breakfast and a meadow view. A large skylight brightens the outdoor room and the interior window seat in the living room beyond.

Located in close proximity to the neighboring home, the McTeigues' home is buffered by strategic siting of the detached garage and office structure, which helps to define a more private entry area. Although conventionally built, the roof detailing, stone wainscoting, and timberframe portal of the secondary structure echo the main house aesthetic.

Hundreds of years of efficient and ecological European wood-heating technology are harnessed in this masonry heater hand built by mason Joe Prinzivalli. Tumbled brick, clefted stone, and cast-iron hardware create an old-world atmosphere. Long after the fire has burned out, the massive walls continue to radiate a comfortable heat, creating a focal point for family activity throughout the winter. A rice-paper screen covers the living room ceiling, filtering light from two large skylights above. The window seat overlooks the east portal and meadow views beyond.

"When our home was nearing completion and I had the construction of my first healthy house under my belt, I realized that we had created something unique. There was an obvious void in the current real estate market for people like Kendal and me. We live a healthy lifestyle, eat a largely organic diet, and practice yoga regularly. We are conscious consumers and strive to minimize our ecological footprint. Yet the choices of homes we saw didn't include anything that reflected those values. As a result, I formed Whole Homes, LLC. Working with Paula's architecture and expertise and Robert's timber framing and knowledge of natural materials, I plan to provide an ecological housing alternative in the Pagosa Springs area."

— Michael McTeigue

A pizza oven and heated masonry bench (not shown) grace the dining room side of the masonry oven. Beyond is the living room's alder window seat flanked by bookcases and with storage drawers below.

ABOVE » A handcrafted Windsor loveseat in the entry foyer invites one
to remove shoes and assorted outerwear before entering the living room.
The air-lock entry is a wise energy-conserving feature during the cold winters of this mountainous climate. Revealed through the custom glass doors
is the masonry oven and a glimpse of the lake beyond.

RIGHT » The white oak floors of the living room give way to an inset of
black concrete in the dining room. The McTiegues chose this dark finish to
capitalize on the solar gain. Scored into tile-sized squares, even a trained
eye could mistake this for slate! Beyond, a thickened masonry windowsill
serves as a plant shelf, seat, and additional heat sink.

ABOVE » While timber frame and ceiling variations define the dining space separately from the open-concept kitchen, the dramatic, curved kitchen countertop of honed granite cantilevers into the dining room and integrates the two spaces. The upper cabinets extend all the way to the plaster ceiling to maximize storage and give the kitchen its clean lines. The drawer cabinet facing into the dining room is a good strategy for making the most of a tight kitchen corner. A generous corner window brings both light and views into the kitchen. The custom-built alder cabinetry complements the white-fir timber frame.

RIGHT » At the dining-room table one can enjoy the masonry oven on one side. Opposite, panoramic views of the lake are captured through an expanse of glass framed by the timber structure.

A Straw/Clay Cottage

PROJECT: Weaver-Hovemann Residence

ARCHITECTS: Baker-Laporte and Associates and J. T. Heater

TIMBERFRAME DESIGN: Robert Laporte

BUILDER: Building with Spirit, Eric Glazzard, principal

LOCATION: Near Nevada City, California

Muffy Weaver and Glenn Hovemann have made a career of bringing the wonders of nature into the hearts of children through their publishing company, Dawn Publications. When they had an opportunity to build their own home they turned to nature for their inspiration. The 2,550-square-foot home is framed with a one-and-a-half-story European-style timber frame. The design reflects Muffy and Glenn's desire to integrate their daily lives with the magnificence of their natural surroundings . . . to be able to sleep under the stars with the sounds of the river below them, to meditate with the sunrise, to repose outdoors and take in the sunsets, to grow their own food, make their own electricity, and to give expression within the very fabric of their home to the many talented hands within their expansive circle of friends and family.

A large north-facing entry portal gives way to a generous entry that shares a double-sided masonry heater with the living room. The vaulted living room provides a distribution route for the heat from the masonry heater to the second floor. A guest bedroom and guest bath are situated to the east and west of the entry. Living room, dining room, and kitchen are open to one another and defined as separate spaces by the timberframe posts and beams and different ceiling heights and treatments. A south-facing sunroom off the dining room acts as a passive heat source in the winter. Doors lead from the sunroom to a generous west portal that overlooks the Yuba River.

Upstairs, a gable roof plan with both gable and shed dormers creates living space in all four directions. The stairway opens onto a north-facing office area. A balcony overlooks the living room and surrounds it on three sides. A sunny master bathroom is in the west-facing gable end. The south-facing master bedroom leads out to a large sleeping porch that captures the river valley views. A meditation room, awash everyday with early morning sun, fits under the east gable.

A Cooperative Process.

We had never seriously thought of building a home. Life is busy enough as it is, and buying a house was more our speed. But then we happened upon some land that tugged at our hearts and made us daydream. It was the land that called us to the task: a large undeveloped piece of land in the foothills of the Sierra Nevadas with Ancient Mountain to the northeast, sloping to a grassy meadow strewn with spring wildflowers and a few clumps of blue and live oaks, then plunging 800 feet down a cliff to the wild and scenic South Yuba River. The land not only had great beauty and vistas but it also had power. We could feel it. It was not yet on the market, but the owner

Glenn writes, "Art needs a good frame, and to properly frame the house and garden, we asked our cob-expert friend, Rob Polacek, to build a shapely, 65-foot-long cob wall with gothic arches on the outer edge of the garden. One passes through a cob arch, then along a flagstone garden path, to reach the front entrance to our home."

needed to sell and we felt privileged to buy. It was to become WildGrace Farm: "wild" because the land is indeed still wild, and "grace" because of how it came to us and because it continues to bless us.

But it was completely undeveloped, so, novices that we were, we turned our attention to the task of building. We knew we wanted something that fit well into the sun-bleached fields of summer and the groves of oaks and gray and Ponderosa pines. We wanted something that would function well in hot, dry summers when there is typically no rain for six months and the temperature frequently passes the 100 degrees Fahrenheit mark—but would also function well during the rainy winters when temperatures would occa-sionally dip into the twenties and thirties. We had a prefer-ence for earth-friendly materials as much as possible: rock, clay, straw, and wood (hopefully harvested at least from this corner of the country). We wanted something that would last for generations without excessive maintenance. And we wanted something that would be cozy and encompassing, pleasing to the eye and uplifting to the spirit.

Never having done this before, we did some very basic research, including subscribing to *Natural Home* magazine and reading the classic book, *A Pattern Language* by Christopher Alexander. We thought back on the houses we knew and liked, such as the round house, or yurt, owned by friends in Oregon. Ultimately we were attracted to the econest clay/straw homes championed by Robert Laporte and Paula Baker-Laporte. We liked how they combined the insulative value of straw bale and the thermal mass of rammed earth. We also liked the possibility of a timberframe structure. So we invited our friend Eric Glazzard to accompany us to Santa Fe for an econest workshop. Eric has been building

FIRST FLOOR

SECOND FLOOR

Muffy and Glenn in the entryway of their new home.

The office has views through the open shutters of the master bedroom and to the valley beyond. "One thing we did not account for is the excellent acoustics—too good in the central area, really, if a busy young family were to live here. We expect that the sound will moderate with additional furniture and wall hangings."

RIGHT » Like an eagle's nest, the outdoor bed is perched above the sun bump with a commanding view of the Yuba valley.

BELOW » The stone foundation and careful preservation of the surrounding vegetation anchor the home to its site as though it had always been there.

for about twenty years. He was interested in alternative techniques, yet had never seen anything that fully satisfied his insistence on quality and durability—until this. The econest seemed solid, down-to-earth. He signed on.

Summer, 2002, was spent on the basics: a mile-long driveway installed by our yogi friend Jim VanCleave. A well, holding tank, and all the associated pipes were installed. And Eric (assisted by our eldest son, Oren, among others) built a shed for firewood, a tractor, and a multipurpose 'barn' that would be a garage with a tool room and a power room. We were off the grid so we put solar panels on the barn roof; more recently, we installed a wind generator as well. Muffy wanted the barn to be a decent distance from the house site, so that's where it went, about 150 feet away.

We engaged Paula Baker-Laporte as our designer, in part because of her familiarity with clay/straw. We each wrote down what was important to us in a house, including things like our wish for a comfy cottage-style feeling blended with the earthy feel of hand plastering and adobe. We told her of our wish to have the house relate easily to the outdoors, particularly the west side where a grove of blue oaks filtered the afternoon sun, and the south side where we wanted to see and hear the river in the canyon below, and the north side where we planned the garden. We told her how we would like a sleeping deck overlooking the river, a masonry heater, and a sunroom on the south. We wanted a timberframe structure—and there was even a veteran in the trade, Doug Lingen of Sierra Timber Framers, located only five miles away.

A portal on the west overlooks the river valley. A large blue oak shades the home from the afternoon sun. The exterior covered porches are multicolored flagstone, thereby accomplishing not only a beautiful surface but avoiding the high maintenance of wooden decks (which are also a fire hazard, a serious consideration in this locale).

Paula suggested an open floor plan above the living room, with the second-floor rooms arranged around the opening. We engaged our architect friend, J. T. Heater of Ananda Design and Construction, to take Paula's design to the level of building plans, and to shepherd them through the county offices. The problem was that in California, sheer values for earthquake standards are very stringent, and there was no engineering data on clay/straw—or even on the knee braces used in the timber framing. Consequently, because of lack of data, those factors counted for nothing, and the engineer required a few metal wall plates to be installed to boost the shear values of the structure. We could live with it.

We broke ground in May, 2003, and with our encouragement, Eric hired a crew that included one construction veteran, a friend and former engineer, Rodric Anderson (Grace Construction), along with no fewer than eight young neophytes (including our youngest son, Naveen). Belted and ready to go at 6 a.m. (sharp!) the crew began every day with a prayer and a song, a clear purpose, and frequent safety-awareness checks. The project ended in December with no construction-related accidents and a first-class product.

We planned carefully for the construction of the clay/straw walls. We decided to invite lots of friends (and their friends) and have a work party! In preparation, we joined forces with Barbara Roemer and Glenn Miller, who are well versed in alternative building, to manufacture a tumbler to mix the massive amount of clay/straw that would be required. Barbara's son, who operates a welding shop, put together a 30-inch-diameter, 10-foot-long rotating drum powered by an electric motor and hydraulic pump. With a little practice, the machine operated perfectly, and saved a huge amount of energy.

Meanwhile, Eric planned elaborately. On the day before the "party," we, along with his regular crew, did a test

ABOVE » Plaster dragonflies seem to be drawn to the light. Elsewhere, lizards and a hare grace the lime-plaster exterior walls.

RIGHT » A balcony leading from bedroom to meditation room overlooks the living room and is surrounded by the warm walls created by adding yellow oxide to the plaster mix. Glenn writes: "To us, having hand-finished and not machine-finished wall surfaces constitutes an important part of the feel of a house. And this is one part of the process in which we wanted our own hands to be intimately involved! Fortunately we are friends with master plasterers, Shahoma McAllister and Prasad Baudeaux, from Oregon, who guided us throughout. Muffy made many test batches before she settled on the color scheme. The exterior plaster was finished with a hydraulic lime that makes it impervious to water. We added burnt sienna coloring to the mix. The interior walls were all plastered with a mix of white clay, sand, and mica, colored with white titanium and yellow oxide to give a natural pale yellow color. We are delighted with the outcome. The interior yellow is light and yet warm, especially when it glows with the setting sun."

run on the north wall. An advance crew of volunteers prepared a huge thank-you lunch. On Saturday, July 19, with temperatures going well into the nineties, fifty-seven people showed up for our party! Many of them were young people networking and learning about alternative building; others were just good friends, pitching in to help. After a demonstration, we organized ourselves into teams. Muffy was in charge of the mixing crew. Their job was to put the right proportion of straw, clay, and water into the receiving-end of the mixer, to be tumbled downhill into waiting bins. Glenn, aided by a spotter in those rather crowded conditions, operated the forklift, bringing bins full of the mix to three other crews headed by Ishak on the east wall, Glenn Miller on the north wall, and Michael on the west wall. Rodric led the crew of carpenters, who were constantly in demand as the slip forms must be leapfrogged up each of the walls as they grow. Another crew organized lunch and made sure everyone was hydrated and happy. Eric oversaw everything. Such camaraderie—it really was a party! By midafternoon, after about five hours of work, 90 percent of the clay/straw walls were complete.

Nine months after groundbreaking, we moved into a piece of art, which is also a very comfortable home—just in time to start a garden!

Was it worth it? Yes, absolutely! Of course there were times when it was overwhelming. All the while, we had a business and (older) children to attend. Yet this home is so inviting—even inspiring—that it is a continual source of joy. We were able to work with so many friends, and to make new ones. In the summer we go to sleep on our elevated deck, admire the Milky Way, and count our many blessings.

– Glenn Weaver

Glenn writes: "As for lighting, there is plenty, but nothing harsh. A soft glow emanates from our choice of alabaster light fixtures (economical faux alabaster—alabaster particles shaped with resin—actually)."

A north-facing entry portal and inset arch frame the "celestial" entrance to the home. It leads to a generous foyer that shares a double-sided masonry heater with the living room. Bright, natural plaster colors; sun and moon windows; and sculpted-clay relief wall creatures bring a delightful hobbit-house feel to the home, which the owners describe as "Southwest adobe meets Northwest forest."

ABOVE AND BELOW » A double-sided masonry heater serves as a room divider between the entry foyer and the living room. The heater core was made by Temp-Cast, of Canada. With glass doors on both sides, it accommodates a magnificent roaring fire for an hour or two, during which time heat is transferred to its enormous bulk. It then radiates for more than twenty-four hours afterward. The heater was finished in stone on the lower part and in hand-finished cob on the upper part. Cob (a mixture of mostly clay and sand, with some straw) is ideal for adding sculpted decorations, and the Weavers' artist daughter, Anisa, shaped an owl in an oak branch on the foyer side, and a quail family above the rock mantelpiece.

LEFT » A colorful wool rug enlivens the oak floor of the living room and both contrasts and complements the yellow tones of the plaster walls. An entertainment center is tucked under the stairway that leads to the second floor. A cozy sitting nook framed under the balcony to the west overlooks the west portal and Yuba River valley beyond.

The Way of the Yogi

PROJECT: Tias and Surya Little Residence

ARCHITECT: Baker-Laporte and Associates

BUILDER: Econest Building Company

LOCATION: Santa Fe, New Mexico

This 1,330-square-foot home is located on twelve piñon-covered acres in Santa Fe overlooking the Sangre de Cristo foothills to the north and east. A raised wooden entry platform wraps around the northeast corner of the building, creating an outdoor space that takes advantage of the views. A sunken entry has expansive glass to the north and east bringing these views into the central living space. The structure is a hybrid with a timberframe core and portal and Larsen truss perimeter walls. The mechanical room is located in an adjacent studio. Water conservation strategies include roof and gray water collection; a 3,000-gallon cistern storing rainwater collected from the metal roof; and gray water from bathing, laundry, and kitchen is recycled into various underground infiltrators, helping to nourish the gardens and natural vegetation.

Creating a Nurturing Home. "As owners and co-directors of Yoga Source, we lead busy and high-profile lives. Above all else we wanted a home where we could rest, retreat, rejuvenate, and carry out our own meditation and yoga practice. We also wanted a peaceful and healthy environment to raise the future family we were anticipating. With our newly purchased land we began to plan our new home. We made an appointment to meet Paula because of her reputation as an architect who was knowledgeable about healthy building. When she showed us the home that Robert had built for them, it was love at first sight. The home's nurturing and peaceful feeling combined with the Japanese-influenced styling was just what we were looking for. We signed up for the next workshop and began working on the plans with Paula. Four months later our walls were raised. We participated in the construction as much as our busy schedules would allow, and then some. Besides choosing all

The subtle combination of burnt umber and iron oxides in the clay plaster harmonize with the simple linens and accent pillows and are a testament to Surya's refined color sense. Wonderful views and the open plan afforded by the timber frame create a spaciousness that extends beyond this home's humble footprint.

of the fixtures, fittings, tiles, appliances, etc., we went to Berkeley, California, to meet and have tea with Walter-san, the artisan who made the tatami for our bedroom. I helped build the walls, stuffed cotton insulation around windows and doors, and helped install and finish the wood flooring. Surya, the colorist in our family, hand-mixed each batch of the colored clay plaster that finished the clay/straw walls.

"The months of hard work paid off as we saw our dreams come to fruition. At the time of this writing we prepare to welcome our first child into the nest!"

— Tias Little

Tias, Surya, and baby Eno a few weeks prior to his first formal appearance.

LEFT » The entry deck, sheltered under the umbrella of a generous roof overhang becomes a place of repose from which to enjoy the Japanese-style entry garden and sunrise over the rolling foothills and mountains beyond.

RIGHT » A formal timberframe gateway invites visitors through a Japanese-style garden to the front door. The finely detailed gate is a glimpse of what is to come. Bamboo and stone echo themes of the garden designed by landscape architect Donna Bone.

OPPOSITE » A spacious kitchen, where Surya practices and teaches the art of macrobiotic cooking, opens onto the main living area. A curvilinear butcher-block island becomes a station for several hands during cooking demonstrations and is always the center of activity at gatherings where Surya's food is a highlight. Surrounded on three sides by views, this U-shaped layout picks up the quiet sophistication of the home's polished black granite countertops, stainless appliances, and sculpted cherry-wood detailing.

RIGHT » Above an inset banco is a piece created especially for the Littles by Chinese master-calligrapher Alok Hsu Kwang-Han. To the left, a corner of the solar space shows the black slate floors and thickened masonry plant sill designed to store winter sunshine.

LEFT » A quiet corner for teatime. Upper shelving displays a collection of Asian teaware.

LEFT » The view through the glazed entry to the entry garden and foothills beyond is again revealed in the living room. The Japanese-style entry banco stores shoes and keeps the entry uncluttered, contributing to the Zen quality of the Little residence. The cherry built-ins and furnishings throughout the home provide a rich contrast to the maple flooring.

Close investigation of this post, and all others in this home, reveals that it is oriented as it was in the forest, standing upright. According to the lore of the Japanese timberframing tradition, this respectful acknowledgment by the craftsman bestows longevity and blessings upon the residence.

OPPOSITE » Horizontal Japanese braces surround and define the living room core. Its rice-paper ceiling is echoed by the shoji panels, which retract to reveal the round window of the bedroom beyond. A simple alter with a black granite sill is built into the central axis on the living room wall.

LEFT » The bedroom floor, with the exception of the maple bed platform, is covered in traditional tatami mats that have a core of rice straw and covering of woven reeds.

LEFT AND BELOW » The black granite bowl sink and countertop, slate floors, steam-shower enclosure, cedar shoji, and cherry cabinets pick up the themes and colors from throughout the home in this restful master bathroom. The sliding shoji creates a private compartment for the commode. The soaking tub, surrounded by glass, looks out onto a peaceful landscape.

LEFT » A granite sink rests on a cherry countertop in the guest bath. In the hands of a craftsman, tree and boulder are transformed from the rough into objects for use. Polishing reveals the beauty of their texture and grain, timeless gifts of nature.

HANDCRAFTED EFFICIENCY

PROJECT: Baker/Laporte Guest House

ARCHITECT: Paula Baker-Laporte, AIA

BUILDER: Robert Laporte, Econest Building Company

LOCATION: Tesuque, New Mexico

This 700-square-foot econest was originally built as a guest house. It is a study in efficiency containing everything that a guest might find in a larger home, but compacted into a 700-square-foot space. This includes the 12-inch-thick walls, leaving approximately 600 square feet of living space. The layout is similar to the Peregrine (see page 68) but shrunk down to "hummingbird" size. We were delighted when Patrick Malone moved into the space and became not just a neighbor but a friend, though we were a little skeptical when he partnered up with Dyan and they began to share the space—we were anxious that 600 square feet, even if very efficient, might be too small for a couple using the space as a full-time residence—but they've made it work beautifully.

Small Comforts.
"This little home has been a sanctuary for me. The clay/straw walls mediate extreme temperatures and provide for a sealed, quiet buffer that provides year-round comfort. My favorite aspect of the home is the organized flow of usable space and the positive energy that the *vastu* design creates. I enjoy different sections devoted to positive uses: an eating area with window seat; a kitchen area; a double desk area; a bathroom; an alter; a socializing/relaxing couch area; a sun space for plants, yoga, and drying clothes; a sleeping alcove; and a mudroom entry space."

— Patrick Malone

No "Stuff" Necessary.
"I enjoy all the windows that bring cheer and brightness to the house. I have access to views and sunlight everywhere I turn. The skylight and sun bump are beautiful features that open up the space, blurring the boundary between indoors and outdoors. Ample cupboards and shelves built into the walls help tremendously with organization without the need for too much furniture. The incredible efficiency of the home has encouraged us to be more discriminating about what is 'necessary.' We have spent a fair amount of time and energy to

A view from the central living space to the dining nook. As in the main house, a rice-paper and cedar screen brings diffuse light into the heart of the space from the sky-lights above. This creates a serene central focus around which activities orbit. The warm, peachy travertine floors and soft ochre walls set a peaceful tone.

Patrick and Dyan outside, in front of the sun bump.

recycle and pare down our 'stuff,' which has been a rewarding and liberating process. We do have a storage unit to rotate seasonal clothing and other items.

"Living in this healthy home has been a catalyst for individual growth and a deepening understanding of ourselves and of each other. The home has been a secure stepping-stone on our path to empowerment as well as physical health and emotional well-being."

— Dyan

The step-down entry with slate tile floors says "Welcome and please remove your shoes here."

View from the sun space to the kitchen and dining spaces. A pantry divider wraps around the corner post, separating the kitchen and the central space. An under-counter oven and fridge free up the solid slate countertops, maximizing work surfaces around the sink and three-burner inset cooktop. Solid cherry upper shelving units provide for accessible storage and are tied together by a display shelf that runs the length of the kitchen perimeter.

Tucked behind a post to the north-west, the L-shaped desk area creates an office alcove with plenty of bookshelves beside and above it.

Framed by a Japanese brace, the queen-sized bed alcove has deep drawers beneath for linen storage. A niche and deep windowsill create space for bedside necessities. While the dropped aspen ceiling lends a more intimate feeling to the space, the bed serves as an additional seating area for the central space during gatherings.

RIGHT » The only interior door in this home leads to the bathroom where tumbled, clefted, and honed slate and travertine are combined for visual interest. A handcrafted travertine sink was imported from Mexico. The oversized vanity doubles as a built-in dresser.

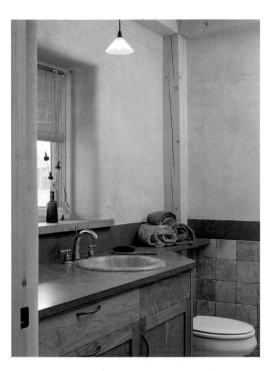

BELOW » The spirit of the home is echoed in this unique Danish table. It can be retracted into an attractive 18 by 30 inch console, providing seating for two with one leaf in place, or expand to seat six with both leaves extended. It has a reversible stainless-steel/cherry surface inset to accommodate hot or cold servings and a well-organized drawer with places for wine, place settings, and cutlery in addition to a hidden compartment! It embodies beauty, efficiency, convenience and flexibility—just what we set out to do in the design and construction of this guest house!

A window seat bumps out to the east, capturing the morning sun. Wrapped by a deep cherry sill and display shelving with drawers below, it creates seating and storage for the dining space.

URBAN CAPE COD

PROJECT: Lansing Street House

ARCHITECT AND BUILDER: Lou Host-Jablonski, AIA

LOCATION: Madison, Wisconsin

This home is located in a post–World War II neighborhood of Madison, Wisconsin. The surrounding houses are modest in size and quality. The Cape Cod–style design is scaled to fit in. Zoning constraints dictated the footprint and location on the lot.

Locating in this existing neighborhood was an ecological decision; Lou Host-Jablonski wanted to be able to walk or bicycle to work. It also meant that the basic infrastructure that supports the home—streets, schools, utilities, police and fire services, garbage collection and so on—were already in place. In contrast to building in a new subdivision or on rural acreage, there was a far smaller environmental impact from building this house on an existing city lot.

Lou kept to a straightforward design and "just-right" size so as to use the minimum amount of building materials—and energy to heat, cool, and light—for a three-bedroom home that will comfortably accommodate an average family.

The home's universal design (also known as barrier-free design) includes such elements as a wheelchair-accessible entry, bathroom, and kitchen, and carefully placed light switches and lever door handles to accommodate the physical characteristics of people of all ages and abilities.

The Main House dimensions are 24 by 36 feet, an 864-square-foot footprint. The second floor is somewhat smaller because the walls are actually the sloping roof trusses. The second floor has about 250 square feet of more usable space under a reasonable ceiling height, with additional generous cabinets and closets built into the areas with sloped ceilings. It is called the "Main House" because it's attached to the tiny 1930s "Little House" on the lot. With the Little House eventually remodeled into a guest wing, the whole will have about 1,900 square feet of living space.

FIRST FLOOR

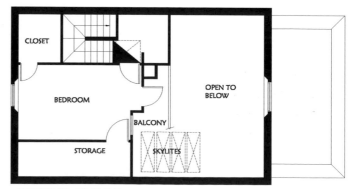

SECOND FLOOR

A view through the length of the home. At right, a large armoire is fashioned from reused doors and straw-based particle board; the wall at left is of sustainably-harvested aspen boards. The ceiling, made of wood-efficient engineered floor joists, is colored with milk paint and lit with integrated compact-florescent lighting. The runner protecting the earthen floor is made from recycled fibers.

The Art and Science of Thermal Resistance.

Lou Host-Jablonski, AIA

"As an architect, building a new home for myself is an opportunity to integrate everything I've learned about combining energy efficiency; a healthy living environment; and ecologically aware, low-pollution materials. I'm able to 'push the envelope' in ways that I can't when designing for a client, and use the project as a research site. I use the house to demonstrate these integrated concepts to students, fellow design professionals, potential clients, and the public.

"Since finishing architecture school in the mid-'70s, I've studied every form of alternative construction I can find— strawbale, adobe, rammed earth, 'earth-ship' construction, and others—looking for a system that did it all. It had to be energy efficient, buildable, low-toxic, and reasonably compatible with modern codes. It had to be reasonable in terms of costs and in terms of availability of materials. It had to be ecologically sensitive and have longevity. And it seemed that each system had some issues that didn't recommend it for use in a midwestern climate.

"In the early '90s I attended a clay/straw workshop in Iowa with Robert. I took the workshop, did the timber framing, clay/straw infilling, and then earth plastering. By the end of

Our air-core floor is a passive solar-heat storage feature. Solar heat from the south-facing windows and skylight is stored and distributed by circulating air through many channels below the floor slab. We're following the basic concepts presented by James Kachadorian in his book *The Passive Solar House*. Whereas Kachadorian uses concrete blocks and slabs to create his floors, we wanted our floor to be earthen, constructed over a base of bricks. Our 5-inch-thick earthen floor contains a high proportion of gravel for enhanced heat-storage capacity.

FPL staffers trimming the samples to ready them for the testing apparatus, which requires very flat, parallel surfaces for accurate thermal measurement.

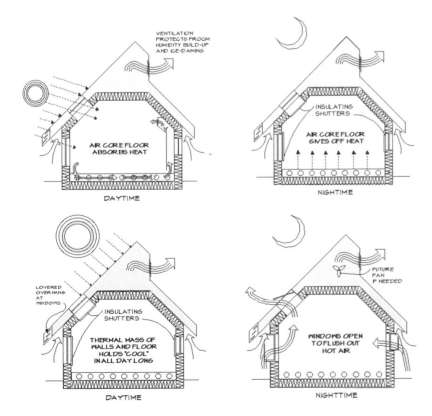

the week I understood this was an integrated family of techniques that worked well together. Robert, who had been doing this for years, was a very conscientious and expert builder, and had done his homework—studying and going to Germany where a lot of these techniques have been developed. In addition, I could see that there were options for using it with light framing, which is even more wood-efficient.

"In 2003, the U.S. Forest Products Laboratory (FPL) in Madison, Wisconsin, performed thermal testing on samples of clay/straw material that our team prepared. Our results concurred with similar tests done in Germany in the 1980s; a less dense, straw-rich mix will have a better R-value than a heavier mix with more clay and less straw.

"This investigation helped us to establish an optimum mix for clay/straw walls for a midwestern-America climate. Clay/straw contained less water and clay, while still achieving a good dispersion of the clay over the straw fibers. The result was durable, solid walls with an in-place density averaging only about fourteen pounds per cubic foot, in fact very similar to uncoated baled straw. Our walls are on the very light—that is, more insulating—end of the scale, with an R-value of 1.7 per inch, or about R-19 for a nominal 12-inch-thick wall. We still have research to do and there is progress to be made, but I remain convinced that it is a family of techniques that really works together well."

— Lou Host-Jablonski

Wisconsin's climate is heating-dominated but routinely experiences several weeks of summer heat in the upper nineties with relative humidity above 80 percent. This house incorporates a passive cooling system that combines carefully calculated window shading, thermal mass, and oversized ventilation channels under the roof, creating a sun-driven thermal chimney effect to prevent heat from reaching the living space. The design of the system, and some sixty temperature sensors placed throughout the house connected to a computer data logger, will allow us to run full-scale experiments to quantify the passive cooling effect.

Reused and recycled materials abound throughout the house and each has its own story. The heavy timber main beam is Wisconsin Douglas fir that helped support a Chicago warehouse for a century before coming back to its home state. Carved stone elements of an old decommissioned communion rail from a nearby church are seeing new service as beautiful front-porch railings. The kitchen floor is inch-thick paver tiles collected by a friend over a decade ago from a demolished University of Wisconsin building. Thick slate-like composite countertops from old laboratory tables came from the same source. The kitchen cabinets were saved from a downtown office building that was being demolished to make way for Madison's new performing arts center—with all exposed particle-board surfaces carefully sealed with AFM's SafeSeal, a low-emissions, water-based urethane coating, to prevent offgassing of formaldehyde.

The structural framing system uses only the minimum amount of wood necessary to achieve a strong structure. All the major structural elements— exterior walls, floor joists, and roof trusses—are laid out to align with each other, spaced 24 inches apart. All the windows are placed *between* the wall studs, so wall headers are unnecessary. Lou eliminated all of the wood normally required to carry the loads over wide window openings, and the extra studs and large headers made from old-growth trees. Compared to conventional construction, he used one-third less framing lumber.

The infill of clay/straw insulation takes the place of the sheathing, bracing the wall studs laterally and providing a surface ready for application of stucco or siding. Using this system Lou avoided purchasing twenty-seven sheets, or 864 square feet, of wall sheathing. His roof and floor framing minimize the use of wood too—roof trusses are made of small-dimension lumber, and engineered floor joists are made from small trees.

The main bathroom, designed as a roll-in shower with a floor drain, has no lip or other obstruction on the floor. This barrier-free design feature allows a wheelchair user to easily move about and use the fixtures. The tiled floor and walls are completely waterproof. The soft cotton shower curtain hangs from a track on the ceiling and stores out of the way when not in use. Sturdy wood blocking is hidden in the walls, ready for the installation of grab bars.

TIMBERFRAMED SIMPLICITY

PROJECT: Robert Laporte and Paula Baker-Laporte Residence #2

ARCHITECT: Baker-Laporte and Associates

BUILDER: Econest Building Company

LOCATION: Tesuque, New Mexico

The home is sited on a high point overlooking the historic village of Tesuque and surrounded by panoramic views. Sunrise illuminates the rolling foothills of the Sangre de Cristo Mountains to the east. To the west, the magnificent Santa Fe Opera House is framed by the Jemez Mountains. Picture-perfect sunsets over the Jemez, symphonies in orange, red, and yellow, are a regular evening event, and at night the city lights of Los Alamos glimmer on the western horizon. Expansive views of the Tesuque Valley stretch across the southern exposure. The beautiful site was a perfect complement to the solar orientation we require on our homes. It demanded that we pay homage to its many facets in the design's conception and execution.

The timber frame defines a square that is 42 by 42 feet. The clay/straw walls weave in and out of the timber frame, creating a variety of indoor and outdoor spaces. In the center of this square is the heart of our home, the living room. Again a rice paper and cedar mandala diffuses the light from two sky-lights in the metal roof above and bathes this area in soft light. The meditation nook to the east, entry to the north, and master wing to the west are all separated from this space by retractable shoji screens. A built-in entertainment center is concealed behind doors.

The north and east entries, the serene central space, kitchen to the south-east, and master bedroom to the southwest are all placements based on the ancient Vedic tradition of vastu. *The main house is 1,880 square feet with two bedrooms and two baths. A separate 400-square-foot guest suite completes the plan and the two buildings, joined by a timberframe breezeway, define a Japanese-style entry courtyard.*

An Econest for Everyone.

"By the time we had lived in the Peregrine (see page 68) for five years, we had 'given the tour' to hundreds of interested and curious people, and listened carefully to what they had to say. Many people remarked that they could easily downsize and that the Peregrine was all they really needed. Many others loved the concept but needed a little more space for a growing family, an aging parent, a home office, etc. The latter represented a majority. We decided to create a home that would introduce our principles of ecological and healthy natural building to a more mainstream audience, filling a wide gap in the custom-home market somewhere between the minimalist owner/builder shelter and the land yacht. We were fortunate in the acquisition of this beautiful site adjacent to our home-and-work compound for our new project. True to form, when the home was completed we moved in to try it on and show it off!

From the breezeway, under the *taiko* beam, through the entry, past the shoji, and into the living room, the eye is drawn to the heart of the home, the Tulikivi. From flagstone to slate to travertine to soapstone, the array of natural stone used throughout the home is all revealed in this succession.

Paula, Robert, and daughter,
Sarah, under the east portal.

"Our previous home was much smaller—1,370 square feet. To bring the footage to 1,880 square feet, we changed a lot of little things, carefully adding space where we wanted it and where we thought a broader market would require it. We separated the shower from the tub. We created a little more buffer between the master bedroom and the living room; we added a laundry room and more master bedroom storage. Our idea here was to take our small-home experience and to apply the same space efficiency and open planning concepts to a modest mid-sized home. We wanted to offer comparable amenity to much larger homes, which are the norm in the custom-home market in Santa Fe, and we wanted to offer higher quality in place of squandered quantity. Included

OPPOSITE » The view into the entry courtyard towards the guest suite. A composition of green, metal roofs creates a "good hat" suitable for the harsh high-desert climate. A cedar-and-bamboo privacy screen completes the courtyard and echoes the Asian detailing of the home. Both the house and courtyard walls are fitted with a good pair of boots . . . stone!

SUITE BATHRM

MECH RM

BED NOOK

GUEST SUITE

DESK

COVERED WALKWAY

BENCH

JAPANESE COURTYARD GARDEN

HERB GARDEN

LAUNDRY

BATH #1

BEDROOM #1

MASTER BATH

SAUNA

ENTRY

VEGETABLE GARDEN

MASTER BEDROOM

TV

LIVING ROOM

YOGA ROOM

EAST PORTAL

REF

MASTER CLOSET

DINING ROOM

KITCHEN

DW

WEST PORTAL

The solar bump-out is integrated into the dining room. A pair of french doors leads to an outdoor dining room on the west for romantic sunset dining *chez nous*. Regionally grown aspen is used to create a quiet texture in the ceiling.

along the way were all the ecological amenities of natural climate control, energy efficiency, water conservation and storage, healthy and natural building materials, etc., that we believe people will come to demand once they have experienced them.

"This new home represents our current state in an ever-evolving quest for refinement of the concepts that we set out to explore. In another few years as we continue to work with these materials and design concepts, our ideal home will, no doubt, be different again. What will we change? For starters, this home is a little larger than we need, the organic food production garden a little smaller than we would like, and our mailbox is still receiving, albeit reduced, utility bills! We are enthusiastically exploring reasonably priced offerings for renewable energy that we can further incorporate into our homes. We believe that making good homes is worthwhile work. Our health, our well-being, and our world view are all deeply rooted in our homes, and ours are made of earth."

— Paula Baker-Laporte
Robert Laporte

An L-shaped covered walkway joins the house and guest suite and forms the main entry. A Japanese-style court-yard captures a bit of lush green and flowing water, and sets up a welcome microclimate to be enjoyed while sitting under the shady breezeway. Surrounding the garden, a low bamboo wall blocks the rooftops directly below and opens up to the sunset views and the mountains beyond. Note the rain chain that moves water from the metal roof to an underground cistern from where it is used to water the drought-resistant landscaping.

This detail of the kitchen shows the open shelving integrated with the timber-frame post. The amber and greens in the recycled-glass dinnerware by Fire and Light Glassware pick up the tones of the plaster, slate, and cherry.

A panoramic view deserves to be captured, especially in the kitchen, so we kept our upper shelving to a minimum. The woodwork is simply maintained with a product containing only lemon oil and vitamin E. The durable slate countertops are unfinished.

BELOW » We both have a meditation and yoga practice. The home is a beautiful vessel for that practice because it has a quiet and grounded feel that is unique to earthen construction. Creating a special place within our home for this practice is important to us. Separated by retractable shoji screens, a raised platform creates a meditation alcove where the beautiful sunrise views grace the home. A niche of cedar, bamboo, and rice paper in the meditation room displays an object of beauty.

ABOVE » The warmth of the fire can be enjoyed from both the dining room and living room with the see-through firebox. A practical feature included in this model is an independent bake oven situated above the soapstone mantel. A hand-forged pendant light over the dining room table complements the ironwork on the fireplace.

The rhythms of the Japanese timber frame are reflected in the ceiling over the living room. The shoji screens create privacy for the meditation room, and when retracted, connect the living room to the eastern view beyond. Simple furniture includes a wool rug and low-emissions couch and chairs. We added local mica and a combination of iron oxides to the finish clay-plaster recipe to obtain our desired color and texture.

Resources

NEW MEXICO STATE GUIDELINES FOR CLAY/STRAW CONSTRUCTION

STANDARDS FOR NON-LOADBEARING LIGHT CLAY CONSTRUCTION:

GENERAL:

Light clay shall not be used to support the weight of the building beyond the weight of the light clay material. The light clay will act as wall in-fill between the structural members or surrounding them.

The structural support of the building shall be designed according to the provisions of the Uniform Building Code (UBC). All loadings shall be as required by Chapter 23 of the UBC for vertical and lateral loads.

The general construction of the building shall comply with all provisions of the Uniform Building Code (UBC).

For the purposes of placement of perimeter foundation insulation, the light clay may overhang the bearing surface of the foundation up to the thickness of the perimeter insulation, but in no case greater than 4 inches.

Unless otherwise provided for in the Standard, the following codes are minimum requirements:

- a. Uniform Building Code (ICBO);
- b. Uniform Mechanical Code (ICBO);
- c. Uniform Plumbing Code (ICBO);

- State of New Mexico Electrical Code;
- L. P. Gas Codes;
- ANSI;
- Current Energy Conservation Code;
- New Mexico Building Code;
- Any additional codes and standards as may be adopted by the Construction Industries Division.

NOTE: The current edition of the above codes adopted in the State of New Mexico with applicable New Mexico changes shall apply. Copies of these codes are on file at the Construction Industries Division.

SPECIFICATIONS:

- STRAW: Straw shall be wheat, rye, oats, rice or barley, and shall be free of mold, decay and insects.

- CLAY SOIL: Dry soil mixture may contain a mixture of clay, silt and sand. The clay content shall be 50% or more of the total mixture by volume.

- STRAW/SLIP MIXTURE: All straw stalks shall be mixed with the clay slip until they are thoroughly and evenly coated so as to avoid pockets of dry straw.

CONSTRUCTION:

- The exterior walls shall be a minimum of 12 inches thick unless otherwise approved by the certifying architect or engineer.

- Light clay shall not be used below grade. The foundation shall be constructed so that the bottom of the light clay wall is at least six (6) inches above final exterior grade.

- A moisture barrier shall extend across the full width of the stem wall between the light clay wall and the stem wall. The moisture barrier shall consist of an ICBO approved moisture barrier. All penetrations through the moisture barrier, as well as all joints in the barrier, must be sealed with asphalt, caulking or an ICBO approved sealant.

- All wood structural members embedded in exterior light clay walls shall be of wood of natural resistance to decay, or shall be treated wood or wood protected with approved coatings, or protective wrap. All non-wood structural members shall be resistant to corrosion or coated to prevent corrosion with an approved coating.

- A moisture barrier shall be installed at all windowsills prior to installing windows.

- A decay resistant sill plate shall be used over the moisture barrier and stem wall.

WALL REINFORCING:

- Vertical wall reinforcing shall be a minimum of 2 x 4s, 32 inches on center, secured to sills and plate or gable rafters. This reinforcing shall be blocked every 8 feet vertically with 2 x 4 blocks placed horizontally.

- Nonstructural horizontal stabilizing bars shall be installed at 24 inches on center vertically and secured to vertical members. Nonstructural stabilizing bars may be one of the following: 1/2 inch bamboo, 1/4 inch fiberglass reinforcing rod, 3/8 inch steel reinforcing rod, 3/4 inch wood doweling, 1 x 1 hardwood, 1 x 2 softwood.

MONOLITHIC WALLS:

- Formwork shall be strong enough to resist bowing when the light clay materials are compacted into the forms.

- Forms shall be uniformly loaded with light clay materials and be evenly tamped to achieve strong, stable, monolithic walls that are free of voids. Light clay material shall be loaded in lifts of no more than 6 inches and shall be thoroughly tamped before additional lifts or materials are added.

- Formwork shall be removed from walls within 24 hours after tamping, and walls shall remain exposed until dry. Any voids present once forms are stripped should be patched with straw clay mixture prior to plastering.

- Whenever a wall is not continuously built, the following procedure shall be used to prevent cold joints: The top of the wall shall be thoroughly coated with clay slip prior to the application of a new layer of light clay material.

OPENINGS:

- Rough bucks and/or door and window frames shall be imbedded in the light clay walls at the perimeter of the openings and fastened securely to wooden structural members.

WALL SURFACING:

- All exterior wall surfacing material shall allow for the diffusion of moisture through the wall.

- Bridging shall be required at the juncture of dissimilar materials prior to the application of plaster. Acceptable bridging materials include: expanded metal lath, fiberglass mesh, tape or burlap. Bridging shall extend a minimum of 2 inches on either side of the juncture.

- Exterior wood wall siding shall be spaced a minimum of 3/4 inch from the light clay wall to allow for moisture diffusion. The siding shall be fastened to wood furring strips. Furring strips shall be securely fastened to the 2 x 4 vertical wall reinforcing.

ELECTRICAL:

- All wiring within light clay walls in residential construction shall be Type UF or approved conduit systems.

- All wiring within light clay walls may be channeled or embedded in the walls, maintaining a minimum depth of one and one-fourth (1-1/4) inches from the surface of the interior of the light clay wall surface.

- All cable, conduit systems, electrical and junction boxes shall be securely attached to the light clay wall or wall framing.

- All electrical wiring methods and materials in light clay walls shall meet the provisions of the National Electrical Code, and any other applicable State codes or standards currently in effect within the State of New Mexico.

PLUMBING:

- All plumbing shall meet all provisions of the Uniform Plumbing Code, Uniform Mechanical Code and New Mexico Plumbing and Mechanical Code, and any other applicable State codes or standards currently in effect within the State of New Mexico.

BOOKS

EARTH AND NATURAL BUILDING

Benson, Tedd. *Building the Timber Frame House.* New York, New York: Charles Scribner's Sons, 1980.

Easton, David. *The Rammed Earth House.* White River Junction, Vermont: Chelsea Green Publishing Company, 1996.

Elizabeth, Lynne, and Cassandra Adams. *Alternative Construction, Contemporary Natural Building Methods.* New York, New York: John Wiley and Sons, Inc., 2002.

Evans, Ianto, Michael G. Smith, and Linda Smiley. *The Hand-Sculpted House.* White River Junction, Vermont: Chelsea Green Publishing Company, 2002.

Guelberth, Cedar Rose, and Dan Chiras. *The Natural Plaster Book.* Gabriola Island, British Columbia: New Society Publishers, 2003.

Kennedy, Joseph F., Michael G. Smith, and Catherine Wanek. *The Art of Natural Building.* Gabriola Island, British Columbia: New Society Publishers, 2002.

Khalili, Nader. *Ceramic Houses and Earth Architecture.* Mission Hills, California: Burning Gate Press, 1990.

Minke, Gernot. *Earth Construction Handbook.* Southampton, United Kingdom: WIT Press, 2000.

Schillberg, Klaus, and Heinz Knieriemen. *Naturbaustoff Lehm.* Monchaltorf-Zurich: Buchbinderei Burkhardt AG, 1993.

Schmitz-Gunther, Thomas, Ed. *Living Spaces, Ecological Building and Design.* Cologne: Konemann Verlagsgesellschaft mbH, 1998.

Smith, Michael. *The Cobber Companion.* Cottage Grove, Oregon: Cob Cottage Company, 1996.

Tibbets, Joseph M. *The Earthbuilder's Encyclopedia.* Bosque, New Mexico: Southwest Solaradobe School, 1989.

Volhard, Franz. Translation by Alice Haller. *Leichtlehmbau— Straw Clay Method,* 3rd Edition. Karlsruhe Germany: Verlag C. F. Mueller, 1998.

Wojciechowska, Paulina. *Building with Earth.* White River Junction, Vermont: Chelsea Green Publishing Company, 2001.

JAPANESE DESIGN AND CONSTRUCTION

Carver Jr., Norman F. *Form and Space in Japanese Architecture.* Kalamazoo, Michigan: Documan Press, Ltd., 1993.

Carver Jr., Norman F. *Japanese Folkhouses.* Kalamazoo, Michigan: Documan Press, Ltd., 1987.

Engel, Heino. *Measure and Construction of the Japanese House.* Rutland, Vermont: Charles E. Tuttle, Company, Inc., 1985.

Futagawa, Yukio, Ed., and Teiji Itoh. *Traditional Japanese Houses.* New York, New York: Rizzoli International Publications, Inc., 1980.

Nakahara, Yasuo. *Japanese Joinery: A Handbook for Joiners and Carpenters.* Point Roberts, Washington: Cloudburst Press Book, 1983.

Parent, Mary Neighbour. *The Roof in Japanese Buddhist Architecture.* New York, Tokyo: John Weatherhill, Inc., 1985.

Seike, Kiyosi. *The Art of Japanese Joinery.* New York, Tokyo: John Weatherhill, Inc., 1982.

HEALTHY BUILDING

Anderson, Nina, and Albert Benoist. *Your Health and Your House.* Chicago: Keats Publishing, 1995.

Baker-Laporte, Paula, Erica Elliott, and John Banta. *Prescriptions for a Healthy House—Revised and Expanded.* Gabriola Island, British Columbia: New Society Publishers, 2001.

Bower, John. *The Healthy House: How to Buy One, How to Build One, How to Cure a Sick One,* 4th Edition. Bloomington, Indiana: The Healthy House Institute, 2001.

Breecher, Maury M., and Shirley Linde. *Healthy Homes in a Toxic World.* New York, New York: John Wiley and Sons, 1992.

Colburn, Theo, Dianne Dumanoski, and John Peterson Myers. *Our Stolen Future.* New York, New York: Plume, 1997.

Dadd, Debra. *Non-Toxic, Natural, and Earthwise.* Los Angeles: J. P. Tarcher, 1990.

Energy Efficient Building Association's *Builder's Guides.* Bloomington, Minnesota.

The Green Guide. New York, New York. *Call (888) ECO-INFO for more information.*

Green, Nancy Sokol. *Poisoning Our Children.* Illinois: Noble Press, Inc., 1991.

Institute for Bau-biologie and Ecology Correspondence Course. Available through Helmut Ziehe, IBE, Box 387, Clearwater FL 33757, tel: (727) 461-4371, www.bau-biologieusa.com.

Lawson, Lynn. *Staying Well in a Toxic World: Understanding Environmental Illness, Multiple Chemical Sensitivities, Chemical Injuries, and Sick Building Syndrome.* Evanston, Illinois: Lynnword Press, 1994.

LeClaire, Kim, and David Rousseau. *Environmental by Design, Interiors: A Sourcebook of Environmentally Aware Choices.* Vancouver: Hartley and Marks, 1993.

Our Toxic Times. White Sulphur Springs, Montana: Chemical Injury Information Network. *To contact, call (406) 547-2255.*

Pearson, David. *The Natural House Book: Creating a Healthy, Harmonious, and Ecologically Sound Home Environment.* New York, New York: Fireside, 1989.

Rogers, Sherry A., M.D. *Tired or Toxic.* Syracuse, New York: Prestige Publishing, 1990.

Roodman, David Malin, and Nicholas Lenssen. *A Building Revolution: How Ecology and Health Concerns Are Transforming Construction.* Worldwatch Paper 124, March 1991.

Schoemaker, Joyce, and Cherity Vitale. *Healthy Homes, Healthy Kids.* Washington, D.C.: Island Press, 1991.

Thompson, Athena. *Homes that Heal and Those that Don't.* Gabriola Island, British Columbia: New Society Publishers, 2004.

Thrasher, Jack, and Alan Broughton. *The Poisoning of Our Homes and Workplaces: The Indoor Formaldehyde Crisis.* Santa Ana, California: Seadora, Inc., 1989.

Venolia, Carol. *Healing Environments: Your Guide to Indoor Well-Being.* Berkeley, California: Celestial Arts, 1988.

Wilson, Cynthia. *Chemical Exposure and Human Health.* Jefferson, North Carolina: McFarland and Company, 1993.

Zamm, Alfred, and Robert Gannon. *Why Your Home May Endanger Your Health.* New York, New York: Simon and Schuster, 1982.

CLAY/STRAW AND TIMBER FRAME BUILDERS AND ARCHITECT GUIDE

BAKER-LAPORTE A.I.A. AND ASSOCIATES

PO Box 864

Tesuque, NM 87574

(505) 989-1813

www.bakerlaporte.com

DESIGN COALITION, INC.

Lou Host-Jablonsky

2088 Atwood Avenue

Madison, WI 53704

(608) 246-8846

contact@www.designcoalition.org

ECONEST BUILDING COMPANY

Robert Laporte

PO Box 864

Tesuque, NM 87574

(505) 984-2928

www.econest.com

EARTHom/BENIGN CRAFT

Joshua Thornton

Box 712

Durham, ON N0G 1R0

Canada

(519) 369-1085

benigncraft@hotmail.com

FOX MAPLE SCHOOL OF TRADITIONAL BUILDING

Steve Chapell

PO Box 249

Brownfield, ME 04010

(207) 935-3720

www.foxmaple.com

GREEN ROBIN BUILDERS

Don Smith

312-1st Street

Crested Butte, CO 81224

(970) 209-5674

www.greenrobinbuilders.com

HARMONY HOME CONSTRUCTION

Thomas Hirsch

Traverse City, MI 49684

(877) 454-7336

www.harmonyhomeconstruction.com

PAUL MacNAB AND WOODY MAGUIRE

RR3

Thessalon, ON P0R 1L0

Canada

(705) 842-5040

RON HAYES

23777 SE Gold Road

Eagle Creek, OR 97022

ronhayes@open.org

TIMBER FRAMERS GUILD
PO Box 60
Beckett, MA 01223
(413) 623-9926 will@tfguild.org
(603) 835-2077 joel@tfguild.org
www.tfguild.org

VESSEY VASTU BUILDERS, INC.
Steve Vessey
2279 Rolling Meadow Road
Fairfield, IA 52556
(641) 472-4118
sjvessey@yahoo.com

VON BACHMAYR ARCHITECTS
1406 Bishops Lodge Road
Santa Fe, NM 87506
(505) 989-7000
vbarch@comcast.net

TOOL AND MATERIAL SUPPLIERS

AMERICAN CLAY ENTERPRISES, LLC
2601 Karsten Court, SE
Albuquerque, NM 87102
(866) 404-1634
sales@americanclay.com
www.americanclay.com

EASTERN STAR TRADING CO.
(800) 522-008
Importers of quality bamboo products.

HIDA TOOL & HARDWARE CO., INC.
Fine Japanese woodworking tools
1333 San Pablo Avenue
Berkeley, CA 94702
(800) 443-5512

HOCK HANDMADE KNIVES
16650 Mitchell Creek Drive
Ft. Bragg, CA 95437
(888) 282-5233
www.hocktools.com

LEE VALLEY & VERITAS
PO Box 1780
Ogdensburg, NY 13669
(800) 871-8158
www.leevalley.com
Fine woodworking tools.

MISUGI DESIGN
3276 Formby Lane
Fairfield, CA 94533
(707) 422-0734
Japanese papers, hardware, shoji accessories.

MUNETKA UOTA ASSOCIATES
163 Tomales Street
Sausalito, CA 94965
(415) 332-0815
Traditional tatami mats.

ST. ASTIER NATURAL HYDRAULIC LIME
TRANSMINERAL USA, INC.
201 Purrington Road
Petaluma, CA 94952
(707) 769-0661
www.transmineralusa.com

SCHROEDER LOG HOME SUPPLY, INC.
1101 SE 7th Avenue
Grand Rapids, MN 55744
(800) 359-6614
www.loghelp.com

SOKO HARDWARE
1698 Post Street
San Francisco, CA 94115
(415) 931-5510
Japanese hardware, house wares, and shoji paper.

THE JAPAN WOODWORKER
1731 Clement Avenue
Alameda, CA 94501
(800) 537-7820
www.japanwoodworker.com

TIMBERWOLF TOOLS
PO Box 258
Freeport, ME 04032
(800) 869-4169
www.timberwolftools.com

VIRGINIA LIME WORKS
PO Box 516
Monroe, VA 24574
(434) 929-8113
www.virginialimeworks.com

WOODWORKERS SUPPLY, INC.
1108 North Glenn Road
Casper, WY 82601
(800) 645-9292
www.woodworker.com

NONTOXIC BUILDING PRODUCTS AND HOME FURNISHING SUPPLIERS

THE ALLERGY RELIEF SHOP
3360 Andersonville Hwy.
Andersonville, TN 37705
(865) 494-4100
(800) 626-2810
www.allergyreliefshop.com
Mail-order catalog offering supplies and building products for the allergy-free home.

ALLERGY RESOURCES
301 East 57th Avenue, Unit D
Denver, CO 80216
(800) 873-3529
www.catalogcity.com (under allergy-related catalogs)
allergyresources@hotmail.com
Nontoxic cleaning compounds and body-care products.

AMERICAN ENVIRONMENTAL HEALTH FOUNDATION

8345 Walnut Hill Lane, Suite 225

Dallas, TX 75231

(800) 428-2343

www.aehf.com

Sells a wide range of household, building, personal-care, and medical products as well as organic clothing, books, and vitamins.

BUILDING FOR HEALTH MATERIALS CENTER

PO Box 113

Carbondale, CO 81623

(970) 963-0437

(800) 292-4838 (for orders only)

www.buildingforhealth.com

Distributor of a wide variety of healthy building products. The owner, Cedar Rose, is also a building contractor who has practical experience with most products sold by the Center.

CASA NATURA

70 W Marcy Street

Santa Fe, NM 87501

(505) 820-7634

www.casanaturainc.com

THE CUTTING EDGE CATALOG

PO Box 4158

Santa Fe, NM 87502

(800) 497-9516

www.cutcat.com

Showroom:

911C St. Michaels Drive

Santa Fe, NM

DASUN COMPANY

PO Box 668

Escondido, CA 92033

(800) 433-8929

Catalog sales of air- and water-purification products.

ECO PRODUCTS, INC.

3655 Frontier Avenue

Boulder, CO 80301

(303) 449-1876

www.ecoproducts.com

Supplier of ecologically sound building products.

ENVIRONMENTAL HOME CENTER

1724-4th Avenue South

Seattle, Washington 98134

(800) 281-9785

www.enviresource.com

JANICE CORPORATION

198 Route 46

Budd Lake, NJ 07828

(800) 526-4237

www.janices.com

Supplier for natural and organic bedding and linens, and hypoallergenic and unscented personal-care products.

THE LIVING SOURCE

PO Box 20155

Waco, TX 76702

(254) 776-4878

(800) 662-8787 (voice mail order line)

www.livingsource.com

Catalog sales of "products for the environmentally aware and chemically sensitive."

The Natural Choice
1365 Rufina Circle
Santa Fe, NM 87505
(800) 621-2591
www.bioshieldpaint.com
Catalog sales of natural paints, stains, and healthy home products.

NEEDS
6010 Drott Drive
East Syracuse, NY 13057
(800) 634-1380
www.needs.com
Mail-order service offering a wide array of personal-care products for the chemically sensitive.

The Nontoxic Hotline
(510) 472-8868 (consultations)
(800) 968-9355 (orders)
www.nontoxic.com
Catalog sales of products for achieving and maintaining indoor air quality and safety for homes, offices, and automobiles.

Planetary Solutions
2030-17th Street
Boulder, CO 80302
(303) 442-6228
www.planetearth.com
Environmentally sound materials for interiors.

PHOTO CREDITS

Audubon Society: p. 9

Donna Bone: p. 11

Econest Building Company: pp. 14; 16–18; 20–23; 25; 31; 32, left, right; 33, right; 35, right; 36; 37

J. T. Heater: pp. 3, images a, c; 42, image d; 85–95

John Banta: p. 12

Laurie Dickson: pp. 3 images b, d; 33, left; 34, right; 42, images a, b, c; 43, images b, c; 53; 55–57; 60; 61; 63–67; 70; 72; 74, bottom left, right; 75, bottom; 77–83; 97; 98; 100; 101–103; 105–109; 117; 119; 120; 121, right; 122–125

Lisl Dennis: pp. 71; 73; 75, top

Lou Host-Jablonski: pp. 111–15

Mark Paul Patrick: pp. 47

Paula Baker-Laporte: pp. 34, left; 35, left; 69; 74, top; 118

Povy Kendal Atchison: pp. 43, image d; 45; 46; 48–51

Robert Laporte: pp. 10; 28; 99, bottom; 121, left

Terrence Moore: pp. 43, image a; 54; 58

INDEX

adobe, 12, 13, 24, 33, 39, 41, 65, 70, 72,89, 93, 112

Baker-Laporte and Associates, 52, 62, 68, 76, 84, 96, 116
Baker/Laporte Guest House, 104–109
Baker-Laporte residence #1, 68–75
Baker-Laporte residence #2, 116–125
bamboo, 16, 18–20, 22, 47, 49, 74, 99, 119, 121
Bau-biologie, 28–29, 37, 68
Boston ridge, 45
brahmastan, 49, 74
building official, 11, 12, 39, 41
"building-related illness," 24
Building with Spirit, 84

California, 84, 90, 98
Canada, 11, 36, 39, 95
Canadian Mortgage and Housing Corporation (CMHC), 11–12
chemicals, 9, 24, 25, 26, 62, 68, 78
clay, 6, 7, 8, 14, 15, 19, 20, 24, 25, 32, 33, 36, 39, 40, 41, 44, 48, 51, 66, 93, 113
cob, 24, 41, 84, 95
code, 12, 17, 27, 35, 39, 41, 112
Colorado, 40, 52, 68, 76, 78, 81
Connet residence, 44–51

design, 9, 13, 16, 21, 26, 27, 30–35, 40, 47, 49, 52, 62, 68, 84, 89, 90, 99, 100,

104, 109, 110, 112, 113, 115, 116, 120

earth coupling, 32, 33, 112
Econest Building Company, 52, 62, 68, 76, 96, 104, 116
Environmental Working Group, The, 26
Europe, 10, 12, 28, 44

fireplace, 52, 56, 61, 72, 124
floor plan, 33, 34, 44, 54, 64, 68, 78, 86, 90, 96, 104, 110, 119
flywheel effect, 13, 33
formwork, 14, 17, 19, 21, 30, 32, 36

Germany, 10, 11, 23, 28, 44
gray water, 35, 69, 96

health, 6, 9, 24–28, 37, 38, 41, 52, 62, 65, 66, 68, 70, 72, 76, 78, 81, 96, 106, 112, 116, 120
Heartwood co-housing community, 56

infill, 10, 11, 14, 16, 17, 96, 112, 114
insulation, 10, 12, 15, 19, 24, 40, 45, 48, 56, 98, 114
Iowa, 6, 40, 44, 112

Japan, 68

Kinkaku-Ji Temple, 11

Lansing Street House, 110–115
Larsen trusses, 16–17, 76

leichtlehmbau, 10–11
Little residence, 96–103

masonry, 12, 32, 70, 72, 76, 80–83, 84, 89, 93, 95, 100
mass wall, 12, 13, 15, 19, 24, 25, 32, 33, 40, 65, 80
matrix, 14, 16–19, 30
McGee residences, 52–61
McTeigue residence, 76–83
moisture, 12, 15, 23, 24, 25, 27, 40
mold, 18, 21, 22, 24, 25, 27, 32, 41
mortgage, 9, 41
mortise and tenon, 30, 32, 48
"multiple chemical sensitivities," 24

natural building, 10, 11, 14–23, 28, 32, 33, 36–38, 39, 40–41, 44, 47, 52, 55, 56, 65, 68, 81, 116, 120
New Mexico, 7, 33, 38, 39–40, 48, 52, 66, 68, 70, 75, 86, 96, 104, 116, 119
New Mexico State Guidelines for Clay/Straw Construction, 39, 41, 126

Oregon, 86, 90–91

passive cooling, 32, 33, 45, 113
Passive Solar House, The, 112
Pattern Language, A, 86
plaster, 7, 16, 22, 23, 30, 32, 33, 37, 40–41, 44–47, 51, 56, 62, 66, 72, 74, 83, 89, 90, 93, 95, 97, 98, 112, 122, 125
plywood, 16–19, 21, 30, 32

pollution, 25, 27, 28, 44, 73, 112
porch, 52, 55, 62, 66, 84, 89, 114

radiant heat, 12, 13, 29, 33, 46, 72
rice paper, 35, 49, 68, 71, 74, 80, 100, 102, 105, 116, 124
roofing, 16, 30, 32–35
Rumford fireplace, 56
R-value, 11, 12, 113

shoji screens, 34, 46, 48, 49, 68, 71, 74, 100, 103, 116, 124, 125
"sick building syndrome," 24
solar heating, 32–34, 40, 45, 52, 56, 61, 62, 68, 71, 72, 75, 82, 84, 112
standard construction, 10, 12, 24, 26, 27, 36, 52, 76
Stanton residence, 62–67
storage, 34, 55, 56, 81, 83, 106, 108, 109, 119, 120
straw, 6, 7, 8, 10, 11, 15, 20, 22, 23, 36, 39, 41, 48, 102, 111, 113
straw bale, 20, 39, 41, 86, 112
sun bump, 34, 58, 69, 74, 75, 76, 88, 104, 106, 120

taiko, 74, 116
thermal bridging, 10, 12, 13, 17
thermal efficiency, 10, 12, 17, 29, 33, 34, 40, 112–113
thermal mass, 13, 32, 33, 40, 56, 72, 86
timber frame, 10, 11, 16, 17, 30, 34–37, 41, 42, 47, 48, 51,

52, 56, 57, 61, 62, 65, 66, 68, 70, 74, 75, 76, 78, 79, 81, 83, 84, 86, 89, 90, 96, 97, 99, 100, 112, 114, 116, 117, 122, 125
Tokanoma, 51
toxins, 24, 25
Tulikivi, 70, 72
"twentieth-century disease," 24
"twenty-first-century disease," 24

University of Waterloo, 12
University of Wisconsin, 114
U.S. Environmental Protection Agency (EPA), 25–26
U.S. Forest Products Laboratory (FPL), 12, 113

vastu, 47, 49, 104, 116
Vedic building principles, 47, 49, 116
ventilation, 27, 32, 33, 35, 41, 47, 67, 113

wainscoting, 32, 69, 76, 79
water, 27, 32, 35, 40, 41, 47, 69, 75, 90, 96, 120, 121
wattle and daub, 10
Weaver-Hovemann residence, 84–95
Wisconsin, 12, 40, 110, 113–114